THE
VICTORY
MACHINE

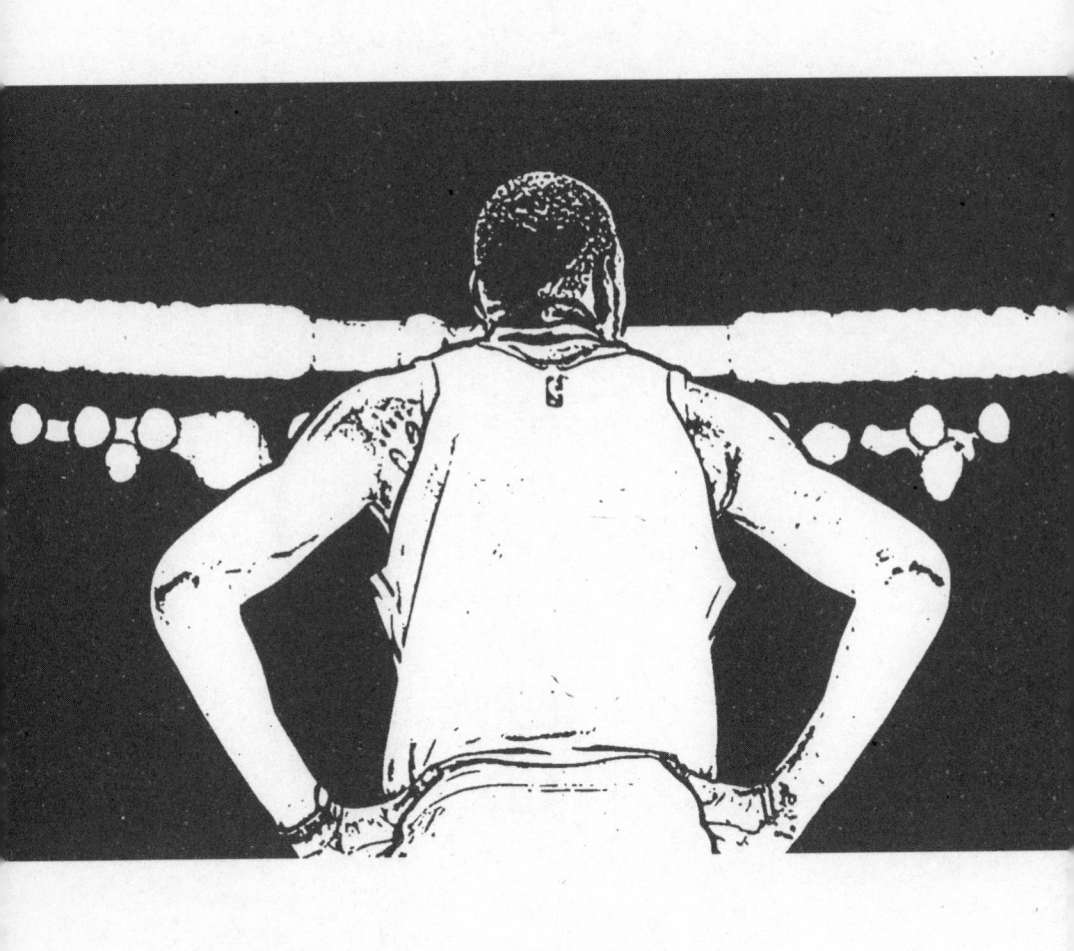

THE
VICTORY
MACHINE

The Making and Unmaking
of the Warriors Dynasty

ETHAN SHERWOOD
STRAUSS

PUBLICAFFAIRS
New York

PublicAffairs
Hachette Book Group
1290 Avenue of the Americas, New York, NY 10104
www.publicaffairsbooks.com
@Public_Affairs

Printed in the United States of America

First Edition: April 2020

Published by PublicAffairs, an imprint of Perseus Books, LLC, a subsidiary of Hachette Book Group, Inc. The PublicAffairs name and logo is a trademark of the Hachette Book Group.

The Hachette Speakers Bureau provides a wide range of authors for speaking events. To find out more, go to www.hachettespeakersbureau.com or call (866) 376-6591.

The publisher is not responsible for websites (or their content) that are not owned by the publisher.

Print book interior design by Jeff Williams.

Library of Congress Cataloging-in-Publication Data

Names: Strauss, Ethan Sherwood, author. | PublicAffairs (Publisher)
Title: The victory machine : the making and unmaking of the Warriors
    dynasty / Ethan Sherwood Strauss.
Other titles: Making and unmaking of the Warriors dynasty
Description: First Edition. | New York : PublicAffairs, 2020.
Identifiers: LCCN 2019038798 | ISBN 9781541736238 (Hardcover) | ISBN
    9781541736214 (eBook)
Subjects: LCSH: Golden State Warriors (Basketball team) | Basketball—Economic aspects. |
    National Basketball Association—History.
Classification: LCC GV885.52.G64 S77 2020 | DDC 796.323/640979461—dc23
LC record available at https://lccn.loc.gov/2019038798

ISBNs: 978-1-5417-3623-8 (hardcover), 978-1-5417-3621-4 (e-book)

LSC-C

10 9 8 7 6 5 4 3 2 1

CONTENTS

INTRODUCTION

THE NBA ARENA IS A FORTRESS UNDER SIEGE. OTHER TEAMS show up, seeking to dominate you, trying to kill you. They want a victory, but not just that. They want what's rightfully yours. They seek to be the ones with the wins, the TV ratings, the cash, and yes, even your most skilled warriors. Their scouts are in your building, probing for weaknesses. Their general manager is talking up your star player's agent. Those two are friends, and they're working to ruin a half decade of meticulous planning—the fortress you've built. Overwhelming success is the only bulwark against their schemes. You must win, win big enough to prevent defection. Because after defection comes the deluge: the losses, the firings, the numbing obscurity. The NBA, a very top-down sport, marketed around a select few superstars, is bleak at the bottom.

This just isn't a normal business, though it might be business at its most base level. It's a Darwinian contest where the company's proxies physically do battle. This is not an industry for the faint of heart.

In a July 2017 *New York Times* article headlined, "The Lawyer, the Addict," a lawyer explains the stress inherent to his profession, saying, "Being a surgeon is stressful, for instance—but not in the same way. It would be like having another surgeon across the table from you trying to undo your operation. In law, you are financially rewarded for being hostile." The NBA is just like that, but with larger sums of money, celebrity, and worldwide scrutiny.

The game is vicious. Basketball is marketed to the public as joyful, but behind the scenes, it's run on hypermasculine cruelty, the kind that has mostly been purged from civilized life.

Here's what I mean, and it's not an entirely aggressive example, just a sadistic one. There was an end-of-the-bench player who had a good run of games. Perhaps he'd finally broken through and found a job in the league. This would mean financial security and salvation from a dreary career in Europe, which comes with a regimented lifestyle American professional basketball players tend to bemoan (European coaches have a reputation for treating their players like hired help).

His locker neighbor was a veteran, secure in his job. So Bench Guy has a poor game. Then another. And another. In response to the third bad outing, the veteran moves a bunch of his stuff into the Bench Guy's locker. "I just needed the space," he says with a shrug. Bench Guy flies at the veteran, as teammates rush in to separate the two. "I just needed the space," the veteran repeats, this time smirking. The implication is clear: You aren't long for this league, so I'm taking advantage of your cooling corpse. In this world, the weak get eaten. Again. Darwinian.

Justin Holiday, Bench Guy, went on to carve out a decent role and stick in the league. Andre Iguodala, the veteran, continued to be hard on every younger Warrior under his dominion. Andre knew harshness to be a teacher. It was classic hazing, really: the kind of mentorship that is acceptable in a cruel business. It was

Andre's bizarre way of showing he cared while also showing that this world is a cold one.

Most teammates aren't friends with one another, despite what you might think from all the televised high fives and daps. Sure, there's camaraderie, something ineffable that I cannot parse in these pages. You'd have to play, I believe, to truly understand what it's like to share a repeated, collaborative adrenaline rush with someone you share no other kind of bond with. But these guys, usually, cannot be friends, because the conditions dictate otherwise. Winning is generally good for all, but your teammates' exploits can easily come at your expense. If the guy next to you succeeds, he gets your touches, your minutes, and ultimately your money. All NBA salaries are public and vary by tens of millions.

There's another factor at play here, something that comes up when you ask teams and agents about their players: many athletes like to live atop a hierarchy, inside a portable bubble. The bubble can be preferable to deep friendship with NBA peers. There's a reason players have entourages, beyond how much they enjoy their friends from back home. It's also that your friends revolve around you. Every day, everyone drives where you want to drive, eats where you want to eat. When you go to the club, you get the hottest girl. That's a given. Sure you'll hang out with your teammates on occasion, but egalitarianism just isn't as fun. Also, sometimes these guys, kings in their own right, have other commitments. The portable bubble, on the other hand, is always available and it's forever telling you that you're better than those teammates. Your teammates never admit to being worse than you. The bastards.

Resentment runs deep, as does paranoia. Everyone is a threat to be ended. Many of these men clawed their way out of desperate poverty and into cartoonish wealth by dispatching one threat after the next. They are under the gun, but wholly cocksure. Their

confidence is earned, validated beyond the wildest dreams of friends back home.

This vibe of swashbuckling insecurity is not confined to the locker room. It infects coaches, general managers, agents, and sneaker executives. Someone is coming for you, but you've beaten all comers thus far. Everyone's primed for a fight and everyone thinks he'll win that fight.

The egos do battle in palaces replete with intrigue. There are twenty-nine NBA arenas (the Lakers and Clippers share one, at least for now), and each is its own little castle, each controlled by a different king. That would be the team owner, often an impatient billionaire who seeks to run the company as a family business. For the Lakers, this dynamic led to siblings fighting over control in a manner only slightly less brutal than Ottoman-era fratricide. In the NBA, nepotism can cripple a franchise, especially since there's no possibility of a shareholder revolt, or other market corrective. A prodigal son can mismanage a multibillion-dollar entity with no recourse, in perpetuity. This is what happened to the once proud New York Knicks, when patriarch cable tycoon Charles Dolan handed the franchise to his son, bumbling blues aficionado James Dolan. The Knicks have been a laughingstock for nearly two decades since, and nothing can be done. All are powerless to stop a man who projects no leadership.

So the king might be incompetent, but the castle revolves around his whims. He must be placated, coaxed, and cajoled, dissuaded from his worst instincts. This is mostly a job for the general manager, the man entrusted to build a team. The GM must foster a good relationship with the owner, for obvious reasons, and also because, sooner or later, his relationship with the team's coach will likely sour. Somebody's going to be fired first, and the GM had better make sure it's the coach. (The average NBA coach tenure is two years.)

Among many other duties, the GM orchestrates player signings and trades, often only to have his owner ruin best-laid plans. Billionaires might know little of their sport, but they demand influence, and of course, the final say. "My fucking owner" is the phrase muttered by many a GM to agents. It explains why the GM cannot do something that's in the mutual interest of agent and GM. Sometimes it's true. Sometimes it's a meager excuse for not doing something they never intended to do.

Player agents act similarly, only they blame their players for bad news when conveying it to teams. In any other circumstance, it's in the agent's interest to project power. Their clients are paying for a man who can move mountains. These agents are shadow figures, men who run the league with fans barely knowing their names. That's because agents are sources for reporters. This isn't a crime, but it mostly goes unsaid: agents had a role in many of your favorite team's choices, and you will likely never be told why or how because it serves nobody's interest to tell you. Some minor player signings count as favors for an agent, a quid pro quo that can't be proven. This is often an investment in something bigger down the road. If your team signed a bad player to a good deal, this may be the unannounced cause.

Agents typically hate one another, and for good reason. There are agents who specialize in poaching players, who swoop in right before the rising star's first big contract, thus snatching up the reward for a relationship years in the making. For an agent, constant vigilance is required. The sales job is never over, the roster is never full, and you never quite lose the status of being both predator and prey. Like every aspect of the sport, only the strong survive.

The strongest influencer of all might be one you're wearing as you read. Nike and Adidas are each bigger than basketball, and thus also hold massive sway within basketball—Nike especially. The aforementioned ecosystems of money, power, and intrigue

might not even be the main event. Everyone in the NBA is work-ing for the sneaker conglomerates, whether they know it or not. Every NBA jersey is emblazoned with the Nike swoosh.

Just as you won't know about agent machinations, so too won't you know about how sneaker companies are influencing your favorite player's free agency. You won't know about these things because telling you about it would shatter the illusion that play-ers are all members of the same team—or at least members of the team you root for. To look at it a certain way, you are watch-ing sneaker salesmen who play the role of basketball players. The competition is real, but the reasons are false. The biggest compa-nies in the NBA universe—the ones who probably pay the most money to your favorite player—don't care about lifting your city's spirits with a win. It's a small consideration next to lifting a multi-national's stock price.

Athletes know where the real money is. Nike reached a $100 billion market cap, largely thanks to their investment in a twenty-one-year-old Michael Jordan. Jordan, now fifty-four years old, makes more in one year off sneakers than all his NBA player earn-ings combined. He's still wedded to Nike, but was estranged from the Chicago Bulls even before he bought a competing team of his own. Superstars show more loyalty to their brand than to their teams. LeBron James is on his fourth NBA team, having gone from savior to villain to savior again in his home state of Ohio, and then on to Hollywood for a new conquest. Through all of that, he stayed true to his lifetime deal with Nike. It figures. Nike boasts the ability to extend his sphere of influence long after retirement, across time and across the world. An NBA team is impotent by comparison.

Now add smartphones to all these dynamics. Like their entou-rages, the hordes of social media followers provide ego boosts to

the NBA stars who are at the center of all this. Social media delivers that dopamine hit, on occasion, but with significant costs to one's psyche.

It can also be a lot for teams to handle. Here's an example, with names and franchise redacted. A lower-level staffer puts out an Instagram story of himself alongside a star player and that star player's girlfriend. Like so many team staffers, he's a man on the make, trying to establish an image of someone rising to a particular echelon. One small problem: The girlfriend isn't the star's girlfriend. She's one of the women he's seeing on the side. The actual girlfriend sees the Instagram and leaves the star. This is now a significant problem for the organization to address and rectify. It just isn't the 1990s anymore. Life isn't so simple because life is so observed, constantly, by a confluence of media and citizen spies.

All of which brings us to the Golden State Warriors. The twenty-first-century dynasty.

The Warriors somehow rose up in this atomized, clownish world, within our modern, narcissism-deformed horror show. It cohered and conquered despite powerful forces arrayed against collective bonding. That it did was a testament to something, or possibly, many things. Was it top-down planning? Was it luck? The fans would prefer the credit be given to Steph Curry and they could well be right.

Whatever its provenance, holding the dynasty together eventually becomes more difficult than building it in the first place. Getting Kevin Durant in the summer of 2016 provided the Warriors with an overwhelming advantage, but at a certain point, the gratifying effects of dominance diminish. There's only so much salary to go around, and money won't fix every issue of the soul.

This is the circumstance the Warriors eventually found themselves in, a familiar one for any dynasty. After achieving so many

joyous victories, they were at a crossroads. They had conquered the ultracompetitive NBA landscape and, at times, rendered all competition futile. Suddenly the Warriors were, simultaneously, on the edge of a Threepeat and on the precipice of breaking up. This is a story of ultimate success. It's also a story of why ultimate success cannot sustain.

1

THE BIG DEAL

EGO AND AMBITION NOT ONLY BUILT THE GREATEST TEAM OF this era, but were necessary for its purchase.

On July 15, 2010, Bay Area newspapers received a curious press release from California's richest man. Oracle founder and tycoon bon vivant Larry Ellison made a surprising non-announcement: he wasn't acquiring the Warriors. It had long been assumed that Ellison was in line to buy the team, then a long-suffering franchise, from then owner Chris Cohan. But something had happened.

"Although I was the highest bidder, Chris Cohan decided to sell to someone else," Ellison's email read. "In my experience this is a bit unusual. Nonetheless, I wish the Warriors and their fans nothing but success under their new ownership."

Fans could be forgiven for some confusion. That day's edition of the *San Francisco Chronicle* included a story entitled, "Ellison Reportedly Close to Buying Warriors." Ellison was indeed close to buying the Warriors. Or at least he thought he was close. "Someone else," it turned out, was, out of desperation, playing by an entirely different set of rules.

Now flash forward to July 10, 2018. The deal has long since been done, and the Warriors' suffering is a distant memory.

"Maybe I should eat something so I can be human," Joe Lacob says, indicating that he just might be in on the joke. The joke, of course, is that Lacob is more machine than man, that he cannot fathom the utility of social graces, that he is a parody of the already parodic Gavin Belson of HBO's *Silicon Valley*.

The other billionaires in the building likely aren't in a joking mood. We are at the Wynn casino in Las Vegas, and Lacob is about to step into the NBA's annual Board of Governors meeting, the league's high court of petty grievances. That ballroom will contain some twenty-odd ownership groups who've no hope for a championship. Men who turned thousands into billions see no realistic avenue past Lacob's smirking face. Joe is lucky that these competitors are merely armed with pens, as Julius Caesar might have encountered a friendlier crowd when he ran into some senators at the Theatre of Pompey. Joe, who refers to himself, co-owner Peter Guber, and Warriors president Rick Welts as a "triumvirate," eschews a toga in favor of flowing white shirts tucked so deep into his 1990s jeans that the cloth grazes the '80s.

Dad jeans or not, he boasts decadent imperial ambitions. "People say we're a dynasty today," he muses. "OK, we've done really well, but you know, there's been some great ones in the past. Our goal is to be one of the greatest teams over a long period of time."

Lacob doesn't believe in drop-off. He doesn't buy into the notion that the NBA is cyclical. His idea is that, when the sun sets behind the Golden Gate Bridge, it's only to temporarily bathe in an ocean as wide and deep as the championship window in front of it. No fallow periods, just Warriors greatness forever.

Obviously, this perspective is insane. But.

"It's the only way you're going to achieve success in life," Lacob explains. "You have to be an optimist, you have to work harder

than anyone else and you have to be looking to the future all the time. You can't rest on your laurels. If we're going to rest on our laurels, all right, we might as well go sit on the beach and call it a day."

At the Board of Governors session in summer of 2016, Kevin Durant's signing was the sore point. "I felt attacked," Lacob says of that session. This time, Joe enters the meeting right on the heels of the Warriors snagging All-Star DeMarcus Cousins for the mid-level exception.

Lacob is animated when talking about the Cousins coup, even more so than usual. Like many CEO types, Lacob projects an out-sized energy. "I have never had coffee in my life," he says with a laugh. "I don't need it! Let's just leave it at that. And I don't take drugs, I don't do any of those things." He speaks quickly, with little pauses between sentences, followed by bursts.

The Cousins signing fits a narrative Lacob likes, as it's a testament to a vision where, for all the Warriors-curbing sentiments at the BOG, the Warriors still remain one step ahead of rules designed to hem them in. "There's a lot of market inefficiencies in the NBA," Lacob says. "Other teams could have gotten Cousins, but they didn't. There's always going to be some sort of opportunity, some inefficiency, I believe."

Believing that you'll keep seizing a market inefficiency means believing that you'll keep outsmarting an industry replete with smart people. Not everyone is comfortable airing such self-regarding sentiments. Lacob is too ravenous in pursuit of the next thing to worry whether the last thing offends. Brash? Certainly. But such brashness is indivisible from the ambition that propelled Lacob into that very ballroom, when no such thing should have been possible.

Before the Warriors were Lacob's, Ellison's purchase had been rumored for years. When Cohan put the Warriors up for sale in March 2010, it was a fait accompli, given Ellison's natural advantages. With $28 billion in a recession-ravaged economy, Ellison should have had a monopoly over the selling process. A notoriously extravagant spender, he claimed one of the most extensive real estate portfolios on earth, to go along with a similarly lavish fleet of superyachts. Even for your average billionaire, entering a bidding war with Larry Ellison was akin to fighting a tank with a bayonet.

Conversely, who was Joe Lacob? A successful Kleiner Perkins partner to be sure, but not to the tune of billions. Nor did Lacob have anything resembling Ellison's fame. On the day of the Warriors team sale, the name "Joe Lacob" had not appeared in the *Chronicle* since 1998, back when the paper briefly mentioned Joe's purchase of a San Jose squad in a since defunct women's basketball league.

Lacob at least had a partner in Hollywood executive Peter Guber, a man of similar capital capabilities. The two had joined forces and grown close while almost winning a bid for Dodgers ownership alongside Frank McCourt, who went on to purchase a percentage of that team later, in 2004. One small catch derailed their joining McCourt. "Frank called when we thought the whole deal was done. Literally done!" Guber says in his office at Warriors HQ, where he's watched over by a massive monochrome photograph of legendary filmmaker John Huston.

Guber projects a similar abundance of energy, but his elocution has more musicality, and is all the more entertaining for his thick Boston accent. There's a theatrical element to it. Guber's words often crescendo as he makes a point.

"Frank called and asked, 'Can you two guys come back to Boston?'" Guber said. Lacob and Guber would meet in McCourt's Copley Square office.

McCourt wanted more money from Lacob and Guber up front. But that wasn't all. Guber explains, "Frank says, 'I would like you to meet the president of the organization.' How can you have a president when you haven't closed the final deal? So he brings his wife in, Jamie." With a laugh, Guber says, "I think, the four of us cannot sleep on one pillow at night! There's too many people there. So that was that."

The McCourts would go on to suffer an ugly, expensive public divorce that would eventually lead to a bankruptcy sale of the team. The bond between Lacob and Guber would continue. And they still wanted a piece of pro sports. Years later, Lacob and Guber got wind of another opportunity.

Guber says, "One day [San Francisco Giants CEO] Larry Baer called me and said, 'How would you like to buy the Warriors?'" This was a thrilling bit of information for the Guber-Lacob tandem. Chris Cohan was selling off a dream scenario and possibly not even in an auction setting. Maybe Baer could facilitate. It was an incredible prospect for a prospective buyer. The bigger the auction, the higher the price, and a higher chance you'd lose out. But if you had a one-to-one deal? Then you could get a team in short order, likely for a fantastic price.

That opportunity was fleeting. Though Cohan may have been relatively hermetic, his phone would still ring on occasion. Often, the man on the other line was Sal Galatioto, a master of running team auctions. "Well, I'm relentless, so I call everybody," Galatioto recalls. "A lot of people won't even talk to me, but I kept calling Chris and he finally took a meeting."

Suddenly, Cohan was in the auction business. "Larry [Baer] went dark," Guber says with a grimace. Baer had to remove himself from any proceedings because there were now multiple bidders and he couldn't show favoritism. In fact, there would be twelve prospective buyers for the Warriors, a "frothy auction" as Galatioto calls it.

It was no surprise that Galatioto wrangled so many bidders for his client. The sixty-six-year-old banker happens to be one of the most quietly influential people in sports. Galatioto is the industry's leading team sale financier. He does it in a boutique, specialized kind of manner one associates with small-scale luxury shops— a Friedman's Shoes, but for sports franchises. Somehow, Sal sells billion-dollar concerns out of an office that employs eight people.

How did Galatioto carve out a niche so massive? Relentless-ness, mostly. The son of Sicilian farmers, Sal shined shoes and worked loading docks as a youth. So many in high-level banking hail from the Ivy League. Sal graduated from Hunter College. He craved a place in the upper echelon of sports business and there was only one way to get it: cold-calling.

Sal explains the process: "Before the Internet, you could buy these books that would have all this information about teams. You would get the general number. You'd call and you would ask for the owner because it would list who the owner was. And I would just keep trying." The success rate on this method was not high, but Sal kept calling.

"Abe Pollin was the first guy to give me a chance," Galatioto says of the since deceased former Wizards owner. "I was calling owners. Nobody would take my phone calls, nobody ever heard of me back in the mid-nineties. And I decided on a summer Fri-day afternoon to wait, because his assistant would never let me through to him, to call him around five o'clock hoping she had left and Abe would pick up the phone. He picked it up, I started talking to him and he said to me, very nicely, 'I've never heard of you. What do you know about sports?' And I said, 'Mr. Pollin, I love sports, please give me a meeting.'"

On the spot, Pollin decided to give Galatioto a test. If Sal passed, they would meet. If Sal failed, they would never speak again. He then asked if Galatioto could name the 1969 Knicks

starting lineup from the series in which they swept the then Baltimore Bullets. Sal said, "Mr. Pollin, not only can I tell you the Knicks, I can tell you the five starters on the Bullets." After Sal rattled off the names from both teams, he'd won a meeting with Pollin, and earned a beachhead into the league. Through Pollin came connections, conversations, and teams to sell in multiple leagues.

For years, the routine continued. Constant phone calls, obsessive checking. With Sal on the case, Cohan wasn't going to simply sell his team to one buyer. Lacob and Guber would have to beat steep odds.

"Peanuts! Peanuts here! Get your peanuts, peanuts, peanuts!" Lacob performs the chant with a wide grin. This used to be his job, hawking peanuts in Anaheim Stadium to pay for college. "I sold peanuts for seven years," Joe reminisces. "Those days you had to sell. You walked the aisles, you threw the peanut bags and you kept the quarters."

The ever-opulent Wynn is a long way from those peanut bag days, longer still from the days that preceded those. Lacob's youth in New Bedford, Massachusetts, was humble enough that he avoids visiting, even when in town for Boston's MIT Sloan Sports Analytics Conference.

"I have a general view, which is that I don't like to look back," Lacob says. "And that's kind of the way I'm built, that's the way I think. I'm all about the next thing, the future. So the idea of going back to my hometown, which was crappy growing up, nothing great, not the nicest place in my mind. Not to say anything negative about that city, but I've only been back twice since 1969, once to show my kids and once to show my ex-wife. That's it. I have no interest in going and I don't want to be near it."

A certain stereotype of the ultrarich holds that the most arro-
gant "bootstraps" types are those who were born on third base and
assume they hit a triple. This highlights the hypocrisy of a certain
cohort, but the truth is likely more complicated. Among the ultrarich I've met, the hardest to humble are probably men like Joe
Lacob, who came from nowhere. How can anyone tell Joe Lacob
anything at this point? "It is attitudinal," Lacob says of his ethos.
"This is America. It's a free market system. You get to do these
things, you get to work really hard."

The current owner of the Warriors is someone who bet on
himself and beat odds steeper than any gambler in the Wynn
faces. And Lacob beat those odds so soundly that in the Board of
Governors ballroom, he might as well be the house.

And yet, even for Joe, there's something to be said for a certain
kind of collectivism. "You probably don't understand this, but in
my industry, venture capital, you never own one hundred percent
of the deal," Lacob says. "You always have partners spelled with a
capital P. That's the way I think and I was taught to think. It's just
better because some of those partners are useful, they can help
you think through things, problems."

Joe needed Peter and not just for the capital influx. Guber offered a crucial idea at the right time.

Guber, who grew up more comfortably in his neck of the Boston area, speaks often of empathy and understanding the plight of
other teams in the league. Unlike Lacob, Guber does believe that
the NBA is cyclical. "I have a different view," Guber says. "My view
is you have to deal with the ebbs and flows."

Lacob only knows one flow and that's forward. Guber has a bit
more feel, more of an interest in what makes people tick. Together,
the two would execute a play for everything. That play came in the
form of a threat, delivered in person.

When it got down to the finals in the bidding process, Ellison versus Lacob-Guber, the latter party was already uncomfortably offering far more than planned.

"When it got to $400 million, it was us and Ellison," Lacob remembers. "I wasn't even sure Ellison had a real bid at 400, I didn't know. There were a lot of rumors that he did not, that he was waiting for me to go away because we needed to go away, we weren't real. We had heard those rumors. So we were there, we felt we could do that. And once it got to that level, which kind of was the walk-away number initially, I said, 'all right, thank you so much.' It was going to take four [hundred million] and unfortunately he had more money than us and he, if he really wanted it, let's be clear, he could've had it because he was one of the richest men in the world. He could've outbid us, no question."

There is simply no way to beat Larry Ellison in an open auction. It was a contest between two non-billionaires and a billionaire twenty-eight times over. This left only one option for Lacob and Guber: they had to give Chris Cohan an exploding offer.

The "exploding offer" tactic has been deployed by many an NBA general manager, some rather infamously: Take this now, or it goes away forever. Take this offer to someone else and it ceases to exist as an opportunity, much less leverage. It can be a bold play, and sometimes a called bluff. But if you're desperate enough, it's the only play that's right. And Lacob-Guber were desperate, after having missed out on prior teams.

How to handle the notoriously shy Cohan was a tricky business. Lacob suggested lobbing the exploding offer over the phone. Guber had to counsel.

Guber recalls, "Joe said, 'We'll call him and make this offer.' I said, 'Man, I'm a storyteller!' That's my whole history, thirty-five years. When you're trying to sign a piece of talent, a big star actor,

a talent, an artist, you have to be there. You have to look them in the eye. You have to breathe the same air. You can't take any edge off your opportunity."

"The key part of the strategy at that point had turned," Lacob says of the ploy. "I called Sal Galatioto and said, 'I need a meeting with Chris Cohan directly.' And Sal said, 'He's not meeting with the buyers.' I said, 'Well, I have to drop out then. I need to have a discussion about whether I could really buy this team.'

"At first Sal refused and then finally, for whatever reason, allowed us to meet with Chris Cohan. And so he said, 'His son has a lacrosse tournament in Baltimore and if you want to meet him, it's going to have to be tomorrow.'"

It was go time. "I had a plane, fortunately," Lacob says. "I got on a plane; I called the pilot and said, 'Get it ready, I'm going to Baltimore.' So we flew to Baltimore. This is where it gets really interesting."

This is not the story that was told back in 2010, when the deal got done. At that time, and for years afterward, it was commonly presented as a simple tale, one where Ellison screwed up, underbid out of cheapness, complacency, or who knows what. The Baltimore meeting was not for public consumption.

Then commissioner David Stern hinted at it a bit at the time, saying of Lacob and Guber's coup, "It wasn't quite cloak and dagger, but it was to a degree." There's an open question as to whether this move was ethical. Lacob and Guber were circumventing the standard auction process, in favor of cutting clandestine deals. Guber rejects the premise of questioning the morality. "There are no rules, but you break them at your peril," Guber says. "Anything that gives you a competitive advantage that isn't illegal, maybe sometimes in certain circumstances immoral, I think is fair game." He adds, "The idea of having a strategy to go at the last piece of the equation, to face the person, is not only appropriate, it is the best

process. To *not* do it would be an act of derring-do of bad proportions." In Guber's estimation, and possibly in the culture of this world, the result is all that matters. "It's binary," Guber says. "You either had the deal or you didn't have the deal."

It should also be noted that, despite confirmation from multiple parties of the Baltimore meeting, Galatioto discounts this version of events, writing via email, "I don't know where you got that, but it is totally untrue. [Cohan] never spoke with Joe. I handled all the negotiations. Whoever told you that doesn't know what he is talking about. He is completely misleading you." When told that more than one source had confirmed it, Galatioto would add, "It never happened! I was getting bids until we signed the purchase and sale agreement. Chris [Cohan] stayed completely out of the process. If they said that, they are delusional. I was the one that ran the auction. I am the only one who knows what happened. There was no negotiated deal and no meeting in Baltimore."

And yet, in the version of events told by Lacob, Guber, and additional sources, Joe did indeed get on that plane and meet with Chris Cohan. Lacob retells, "I said in the meeting with Cohan, 'I can't bid against Larry Ellison. We just can't do that. So can you name a price that you will sell it to me for. Just name the price.' And we're in at four hundred, which we thought was a lot, and I'm sure Larry [Ellison] did too. And Cohan said, 'I can't do that, we have a process, a bidding process, blah, blah, blah.'"

It was time for Joe to add some pressure.

"I said, 'Well, here's the deal—I'm not bidding anymore, so I'm out. I can't beat him in a bidding process. But if you give me a price that you absolutely will take, I will give you an answer yes or no.'"

All a great plan in theory. In practice, it initially appeared to fail.

"Cohan did not accept this at first," Lacob recounts. "I told Peter as we're flying home, I said, 'I don't think we're going to get

it.'" All that work, all that preparation, had led to another impasse, another stymied effort at buying a team. Or so it seemed.

"The next day, they called me back, and his people said, 'It's decided. He likes you.'"

In theory, "like" shouldn't have much to do with this process. In practice? A team sale is an unusual business, complicated by sentimentality, cronyism, and the reality that everyone involved is usually rich enough not to need the absolute best price. Guber had been on the wrong side of that dynamic back when he'd put together what seemed like an unimpeachable bid for the A's.

"I made the whole deal with Billy Beane, making him president of the team," Guber says. "Billy came to my house, negotiated the whole deal. All fully finished. All fully organized except for Major League Baseball. Then Bud Selig said, 'Sorry I can't approve you.' He said, 'You're okay, but we can't approve you because we're going to do contraction. We're going to contract Minnesota and Oakland.' But it wasn't contraction. It was concoction. It was, really, I think, that he wanted Lew Wolff, who was his roommate in college, to get the team."

This illustrates another layer of complication in a team sale process: is it the commissioner or the seller who holds the cards? Some knowing parties have speculated that Ellison miscalculated and fostered more of a connection with Stern than with Cohan. While, say, longtime NBA executive Clay Bennett might have benefited from a tight relationship with Stern in his pursuit of the then Sonics (now the Oklahoma City Thunder), every one of these situations is different. Stern, though famously powerful, saw himself as more of a facilitator in this and other proceedings.

"I knew that Sal was representing the product, and I knew Joe, and I knew Larry [Ellison] and so I was in touch with them," Stern says in a phone interview. "I don't wanna get any further than that." Stern adds his assessment: "Larry could've made the

purchase, but he didn't. He skipped a beat and Joe moves right in and took the team away from him."

If Ellison didn't have much of a relationship with Cohan, it would have been hard to entirely fault him, given Cohan's status as something of a Keyser Söze of failure. Shamed by bad press, the former Warriors owner had not made a public appearance in years. Few who worked for him could provide me any details on his current status. Only one person provided so much as a phone number. The call was not returned.

Lacob had laid the groundwork with Cohan, though, having met with the man at AT&T Park years earlier. At the time, Cohan wasn't selling, but Lacob wanted to make an impression.

"So he liked me maybe," says Lacob, who then muses, "I think that part of it was that he really didn't want Larry to get the team, perhaps."

A source close to Chris Cohan says that Cohan's wife, Angela, disliked Ellison and had influence over the ultimate decision. If that dislike proved decisive, it's a reminder of how much of history gets determined by little-known actors. Few if any Warriors fans know who Angela Cohan is. Without her, a dynasty may never have risen in Oakland.

Lacob, of course, had his own influence over the proceedings. Having established a positive rapport, Joe sought to make a hard sell to Chris.

"'OK, what's the price?' I asked," Lacob recalls. "He said, '$440 million and there will be no deductions for anything you find during the due-diligence process. That's the price, flat out, has to be it. Second, $20 million, nonrefundable under any circumstances.' Now, that is a risk.

"And so I gave him an answer, instantaneously, and I don't know where it came from, but it just came out of me: 'I won't do that.' And he said, 'OK.' And I heard a silence at the other end of the line."

The silence lingered.

Joe then broke in with, "But I will pay you $450 million, but there will be deductions for something we find absolutely by common business deal transaction standards." Lacob additionally committed to the $20 million nonrefundable up front.

Lacob just had one other big, unusual demand: he needed a signed purchase agreement within seventy-two hours. Such arrangements usually take months, but Lacob pressed on. There was too great a fear of Ellison catching wind and blowing the offer out of the water. Sure, Cohan could orally agree to this deal, but what if Ellison pulled an extra hundred million out of his couch cushions? Could Cohan be trusted not to buckle?

"We worked straight, seventy-two hours," Lacob recalls. "I said to our lawyer, 'You do not go to sleep until this thing is done. 'Cause this is the key, we have to get this closed, we can't have a nonbinding agreement 'cause we'll get reshopped.'"

Three sleepless nights later, the Warriors were secured, taken right from under Ellison's nose. Guber celebrated at his Los Angeles–area home, while holding the "Ellison Reportedly Close to Buying Warriors" story up in the air. Lacob, on vacation in Greece, exalted while strapped in a helicopter flying over the Oracle at Delphi. He even allows some reminiscing for this one. "We took off up there and took our vacation days," Lacob says. "That was a pretty big moment that you like to remember. And pretty fun when you think about it. That was a big moment."

That moment was the start of a dominant dynasty. Many fans might prefer to know less about it. Nobody likes owners, frankly, even if they have some of the same personality tics and drives as top players. It can be preferable to think of the NBA as wholly determined by athletes. It can be comforting to think of the Warriors as something Steph Curry built on his lonesome.

Such fans would not be alone in wanting to avoid this particular narrative. Cohan wasn't wholly happy with the end result, either. According to sources, Cohan was angered by Guber announcing at his and Lacob's official introductory press conference as owners, "We're not the cure for cancer, but we might be the cure for Cohan."

"I sent him a note," Guber says of the blowback.

When recently asked about the events of 2010, Larry Ellison's representation quickly declined comment. In the aftermath of Lacob buying the team, Lacob alleges that Ellison tried to sabotage the process, beseeching Lacob's investors to pull out. "I know, I talked to investors along the way," Lacob says. "I wasn't in those conversations, so I don't know. But I do know that we had a hard time because we thought we had several investors in the deal who disappeared suddenly." Big-money minority owners who'd pledged loyalty to Ellison dropped out during that process. They've thus lost out on the massive windfall that's come with this Warriors rise. Back in 2010, $450 million was a record price for a North American sports franchise. Now? No less an expert than David Stern said of the current Warriors, "The team is probably worth something in excess of $2 billion, substantially in excess of $2 billion, eight years later."

That's a win for the exploding offer, even before adding in all the nonmonetary benefits that come with owning the Warriors almost a decade later. As Stern himself pointed out, the team's 2019 move to the Chase Center in San Francisco appeared likely to ramp up those benefits, even if the Warriors are no longer a seventy-three-win juggernaut.

The not-too-distant past has informed this franchise's rapidly evolving future. So much of what's gone right about the Warriors can be traced to a decision finally made by Chris Cohan, the main

source of everything that had gone wrong prior. The story of Lacob and Guber seizing control of the Warriors is also the story of a team, awful for eons, coming full circle. Coming full circle is a nice, Guber-esque sort of narrative. That is, unless you're Larry Ellison, who was cut out of the loop.

When the Warriors were sold, the underdog won. The underdog then oversaw the birth of the ultimate overdog, the team that would ruin basketball.

2

LIGHT-YEARS

What philosophies defined the Warriors from the top down? Were they incidental to success? Put another way, were the Warriors lucky or were they good? Or was the run just fueled by a desperate kind of hunger that transcended theory?

There's a *Mad Men* scene where a frenetic Don Draper pitches Dow Chemical. He's worked up, channeling an almost animalistic hunger. He scoffs at his prospective clients' declared happiness with their market share, informing them, "Happiness is that moment before you need more happiness." He closes strong with, "I won't settle for fifty percent of anything! You don't want most of it, you want all of it, and I won't stop until you get all of it!"

Lacob has that kind of monopolistic zeal, or at least aspires to. He does not play the game to compete so much as he plays it to end competition. Since acquiring the team, he has been quite open about the fact that he wants the Warriors to be a dynasty forever, much to the chagrin of the employees who work under him. So what if his own number two, Warriors GM Bob Myers, told him the sport is cyclical, that there are necessary fallow periods? Those

were other teams. Why couldn't the Warriors be sui generis? Why couldn't they crush the league in a manner unprecedented, in perpetuity? Why not? This was an insane perspective, but it informed the Warriors' rise from the top down.

Lacob regularly watches *First Take*, ESPN's theatrical, chest-pounding debate show. The daytime sports joust isn't exactly geared to the white-collar set, but Stephen A. Smith and company at least have one venture capitalist completely hooked. He loves few things more than hunkering down and watching sports pundits bellow until the spittle flecks fly. There's something in the bombast that appeals to him. He likes watching guys who believe in the near mystical power of their own opinions.

"He does believe to an extent, and this is going to sound hilarious—" Joe's son, the assistant GM Kirk Lacob, pauses on the thought he started, smiling at his father's manner. "But in some ways he believes in the LaVar Ball philosophy of speaking things into existence. He will probably use a different term than that, but the reality is, he does believe in the power of positive reinforcement. If you believe something fervently enough, there's a chance it's going to happen. If you don't, you're never going to have the intestinal fortitude to make those things happen."

Joe Lacob bought the Warriors and things started to happen. Along with the championships, Joe became a lightning rod of backchannel scorn. He is among the league leaders in "this fucking guy," though Lakers GM Rob Pelinka likely outpaces him. In an April 2016 *New York Times Magazine* profile, Joe Lacob infamously said, "The Warriors were light-years ahead of probably every other team in structure, in planning, in how we're going to go about things."

Many around the league either fumed or rolled their eyes at that level of boastful arrogance. Lacob would later express to me that he had not expected that quote to be used. He was annoyed

in part because the quote pertained to the business and not the basketball side. These distinctions matter, given how perpetual winning is more difficult than, say, perpetually competent ticket salesmanship. Still, the quote defined Joe, if not the Warriors overall. And, while Lacob might not have liked the use of such quotes, and while the quotes did not "flatter" him per se, they reflected a true depiction in a sense. "Joey Lightyears" (as he was occasionally called in online circles) was a caricature, but then again so too was the man. He was a fictional archetype of the Silicon Valley arch capitalist, who just happened to take center stage as his region rose into economic preeminence and became a magnet for East Coast envy. Joe was easy to hate in part because his team and its adjacent tech boom were hard to ignore.

At least Lacob wasn't conveying false humility. Yes, Joe Lacob often comes off as an asshole, but his brand of grandiosity also comes without much pretense. I hear enough from these other techlords who pretend to be benevolent while selling your data to manipulators and extortionists. Give me Office Park Daniel Plainview, telling his struggling competitors that "we're light-years ahead." The phrase is patently dorky and still lands with the force of Godzilla jumping off the Salesforce Tower.

I have more tolerance for Joe Lacob than many of the people who compete against and work for him. If I'm honest, I enjoy Lacob. I find amusement in what might be otherwise deemed unpleasant. The NBA is an entertainment business and Lacob happens to be accidentally quite entertaining.

Whenever he's interviewed, it's gold. That's perhaps not the best heuristic for determining whether you're a good person. Reporters will appraise players as "great guy, terrible quote." There can be a correlation. Assholes sometimes make for better quotes. Great guys fear the reverberations of their words, how those words might complicate interpersonal dynamics. Joe ain't thinking about

that. He's saying, "It's not just Steph," when explaining his team's success and only later, likely at the behest of someone else, coming back to apologize to his superstar point guard.

In-person interactions go similarly. I once talked politics with Lacob, right after the 2016 election. He hadn't voted for Trump, but identified as a Republican voter. "When you make a lot of money, they try to take it," he said. "You wouldn't understand," he added, quite dismissively, and then walked over somewhere else without announcing the need to leave. Joe Lacob's favorite book is *The Fountainhead* and he acts like it. His hypoallergenic dogs are named after Ayn Rand protagonists. I'd guess they spend about as much time thinking about poor people as their owner does.

If it is easy to root against such an individual, that's not such a far leap from wanting to deny him his due credit. In Lacob's case, some simply won't do it, and that applies to fans, former employees, and media alike. It's too tempting to dismiss an owner's influence when that influence is so subjective, far more so than a player's statistically chronicled impact. We don't tend to care about owners unless they repeatedly thrust themselves into the spotlight like Mavericks owner Mark Cuban, or preside over decades of big market failure like James Dolan. Otherwise, the public mostly prefers to act as though the sport's monopoly men don't exist. Fans want players to be the reason for their joy and sometimes coaches. Rich guys who call themselves "owner"? Not so much.

"I hate that term," Lacob once told me of the "owner" appellation, with a grimace. It's fallen out of fashion in the league, given the racial connotations. Adam Silver has suggested that the NBA move away from the term. The annual meeting of owners is now called the Board of Governors.

Yet the term persists in colloquial use, perhaps because it forcefully conveys the power of the position. The impact might be abstract but ownership is probably the most important aspect of a

franchise. It rules all the others. That's the paradox of ownership: your power is as absolute as it is invisible. Does any fan have an understanding of what an owner does beyond "spend money"? How many owners even know? There isn't a manual on doing such a job. It's just obvious when the job is being done badly.

I happen to think Joe Lacob is less incidental to the operation's success than many around the league might concede. Fact: when Lacob bought the Golden State Warriors on July 16, 2010, the franchise was a civilizational blight. Okay, perhaps that isn't a fact, but it is a fact that Oracle Arena became then coach Don Nelson's favorite dive bar besides Smitty's on Grand Avenue. Metaphorically of course. Fact: five seasons later, the Warriors won their first championship in forty years.

Under Cohan, the organization spends fifteen years mired in misery, save for one glorious playoff upset. Then, after they change ownership, they quickly ramp up into becoming a historic dynasty. Was this all just a grand coincidence? It would have to be a hell of one.

The team's road to glory was full of unexpected turns and near misses. It starts, inevitably, with Steph Curry.

Even if the Warriors will gladly build a Curry statue when he finally hangs up his dowdy Under Armour sneakers, they weren't bought in at the beginning. What Steph became—an era-defining player, almost certainly the best shooter in the history of the game—is prized and celebrated, but nobody claims to have seen it coming. He was a nice kid, impressive in his manner. He just happened to be too small and frail for the liking of Lacob, at least initially.

Joe Lacob, not a large man himself, likes the idea of collective size. He said this to me once in the food line of the Dallas Mavericks media room, just before PR head honcho Raymond Ridder popped into the conversation, holding a meal ticket. "Need

another meal ticket?!" Ridder asked, cheerily. "He knows I don't need one," Lacob said with a laugh. "He's just making sure I don't get myself in trouble." Lacob smiled and quipped at Ridder, "That's why I didn't fire you!" Ridder chuckled nervously. Lacob went on to gush about then starting small forward Harrison Barnes's size, alongside many of the other foundational pieces. If this was a team-building lodestar, it's a miracle that Steph Curry survived the cuts of the early Lacob years.

Dismissals at all levels comprise a huge part of the incoming owner's first job. Taking over an organization typically means looking for and excising the sources of its failure. There is an uncomfortable stretch where everyone on staff knows they're being assessed for the chopping block. Long-tenured and long in the tooth coach Don Nelson was fired immediately. Scouts were let go. The real bloodbath happened on the business side, though. Lacob was more interested in purging the sales and marketing aspects of the Warriors than in immediately reorganizing basketball operations. Lacob forged his success in business and thus had stronger opinions about what to do there. The basketball side is a bit more opaque, left to experts.

In the NBA, there is a division between business and Ops, with many from the former desperately trying to infiltrate the latter. This became an issue at a gym next door to the Warriors' Oakland facility where staffers of all stripes used to play pickup. Eventually, Warriors Ops men grew tired of the spot in part because so many business-side guys would attempt to ingratiate themselves during the games. The pickup games moved to the Warriors practice court, a place at a remove from the business side.

Given that division, one in which Ops towered over business in prestige, prioritizing the business side might have been a curious strategy. Doubly so, considering how the Warriors' issues were thought to be mostly basketball related. It was something

like an organizational broken window theory, as dictated by venture capitalists. Lacob believed that incompetence on the business side and elsewhere informed a general lack of cohesion. In September 2011, the well-regarded Rick Welts was brought on from the Phoenix Suns to be chief operating officer. He would soon be tasked with the herculean goal of building a basketball arena in San Francisco, a task he would complete.

In April 2011, the Warriors hired thirty-six-year-old Bob Myers, a successful agent who was unproven in the world of team operations. While Myers wasn't officially the GM yet, he would be named such within twelve months. On the other end of the age and gravitas curve, in May 2011 Jerry West, perhaps the greatest executive in NBA history, was hired as a consulting board member. West would not live in the Bay Area, but he would watch a ton of NBA League Pass and give opinions that drew off a vast well of experience.

The Myers hire was inspired for a new ownership group, but the start was shaky. When the Warriors burned a valuable "amnesty provision" in a failed pursuit to sign DeAndre Jordan, one of Myers's former clients, few around the league were confident in the team's upward trajectory.

Myers's initial roster moves were size conscious, and it wasn't just because he was hewing to his owner's preferences. "I love size," Myers said when asked over the phone about his basketball philosophies. "It's interesting because we're now known for small ball. I don't like small, but I don't necessarily think we're small. I don't know why size isn't valued more. The basket is ten feet tall. That's the concept. It's not changing. The closer you are to that, the closer you are to a passing lane, the closer you are to the rim. The longer you can reach—all those things are highly valuable in a sport that aims for ten feet on every possession." "Prioritize size" isn't the most profound of theories, but there is a value in embracing the obvious.

The draft, as much as anything else, built the Warriors dynasty from within. When you ask former and current staffers what unleashed basketball greatness in the Bay, they cite the historical aberration of a two-time MVP on a relatively cheap, injury-inspired contract, combined with the skill and luck of their draft war room. With input from Myers, Jerry West, Kirk Lacob, now assistant GM Larry Riley, former assistant and current Atlanta Hawks GM Travis Schlenk, and other staffers, the Warriors kept hitting home runs, outside of the Top 5 pick range.

As a matter of drafting philosophy, other than prioritizing size, the Warriors employed an organized rankings approach. "We would rank players at top twelve of their respective position and then we'd take that top twelve and apply it to an overall sixty," one former staffer said. "This was a way of organizing overall quality versus individual need. It was a systematic approach that would have some live feedback of how the draft was corresponding to our rankings." Around draft time, the war room seemed something like a writers' room on a daily current events TV show. News of the day on the various draft picks were bandied about and debated. Opinions were aired, arguments were had, and the end intellectual product was in a constant state of flux and refinement.

In the summer of 2011, after he was scouted by Larry Riley and Patrick Sund, the Warriors brain trust selected Klay Thompson, a large shooting guard out of Washington State. There was some controversy within the Warriors Basketball Ops over taking the kid, given his marijuana possession conviction and subsequent college game suspension. While it's less true these days, there remains a deep suspicion of weed within the broader Ops jockocracy. It can't all be dismissed as an old fogey mentality either, though it's tempting to condescend to hard-drinking scouts who

fear reefer madness. There are smart, young, progressive Ops men who favor continued marijuana testing in the league. The scouting trail is replete with stories of gifted players who fell into legendary marijuana habits and never quite got it together. Perhaps these players just would have found a different, worse substance. There's certainly no shortage of alcoholism in the league, for instance. Booze is tougher on the body, but absent evidence of dramatic misuse, it is more accepted by scouts as an after-hours hobby. Klay might have fallen in the draft due to the pot stigma, a stigma that still exists but is ebbing in power.

In the end, the pro-Klay factions, which included Jerry West, won. Already knighted as perhaps the greatest GM of all time, credit tended to roll toward West in his supplementary consultant role. While West did, indeed, correctly back a fellow shooter in Klay, he benefited from a kindly sort of hindsight. It's less known, or cared about, that West desperately wanted Dion Waiters in the next draft. Dion, full of moxy but not the most eventually efficient pro, was a West kind of guy.

It was initially difficult to know whether West and the pro-Klay factions were right about the selection. In his rookie year, Thompson shot the three well, as advertised, but was less efficient elsewhere. It was at least clear that Klay loved the game with a kind of myopic devotion. Beyond basketball, his dog Rocco, and "dating," there wasn't much Thompson filled his life with. Former Warriors PR man Dan Martinez once noted that Klay was the only player who showed up to the annual media day press conference event and actually started dribbling a basketball. The game was his lodestar.

Former Warriors assistant coach Darren Erman worked with Klay extensively early in his career, mostly on building up Thompson's widely praised defensive game. Erman was effusive in his praise for Klay's diligence, but also his savant-like focus. "He

would have been an incredible army sniper," Erman said of Klay's ability to tune out noise and execute. "He does what you say to a T, will shoot this guy in his left fucking eye, and kill him within the letter of the law without thinking much about it. You say, 'Klay, I want you to force Tony Parker left and mix in going under on screens' and he would do it every single time.'"

Klay took the sniper's narrow lens, which coaches and teammates found to be endearing. Sure he was late to practice sometimes, but nobody doubted his commitment or questioned the primacy of basketball in his life. And anyway, everyone knew that the man's focus could get monopolized for stretches. Former Warriors assistant coach Luke Walton once quipped that, in Memphis, where Klay loved a particular breakfast omelette, "Every step out of this shootaround he's thinking, 'Omelette, Omelette, Omelette.'"

It was all part of Klay's minimalist zen. Erman relayed a story about Klay's literal interpretation of Bob Myers's advice. According to Erman, Klay once told him, "Remember that time that Bob [Myers] said, 'You have to look at yourself in the mirror and don't blame others?' Well how come everyone's doing what Bob said not to do? Everyone's blaming others." Erman, who would later get axed for secretly recording a conversation among assistant coaches whom he believed were deliberately undermining him, had to give Klay an explanation about humanity and its messy foibles.

The 2012 NBA Draft would prove to be a momentous one for the organization. Small forward Harrison Barnes was selected in 2012 with the seventh pick. Earlier in the draft process, the Warriors had looked into taking center Andre Drummond, but he had been awful in workouts. Instead, the Warriors would select another bruising big man, Festus Ezeli, at the end of the first round.

Barnes had been the top prospect in the world before his two seasons at UNC. In those college seasons, he didn't quite validate

the billing. Harrison certainly looked the part, and, in a workout setting, could leap higher than anyone. His character was praised. His work ethic was lauded. He was a noticeably smart kid. He didn't touch alcohol.

And yet, these qualities never really coalesced into stardom. Barnes was an NBA rotation player, certainly, and at a valuable position to boot. He was an important part of the first great Kerr-era teams. The Dallas Mavericks would go on to pay him $95 million over four seasons. The Sacramento Kings would commit $85 million on another four-year deal. Ultimately though, despite possessing the talent and work ethic to command massive salaries, Barnes just lacked a certain unifying feature to his game. Jerry West once put it more bluntly to me, after watching a practice in 2015: "Feet are all fucked up, moves are slow." When I asked West about the possibility of paying Barnes in excess of $20 million a year, the West Virginian took a look at the elevator and slowly waved his hand with a languid panache. "Bah-bye."

Perhaps what Barnes lacked just couldn't be taught. Warriors assistant coach Bruce Fraser once told me a story about teaching basketball in Japan. Over there, players could run a play magnificently, better than Americans could do it. Where the Japanese players struggled was when plays broke down. For whatever reason, they lacked the American game's improvisation within chaos. Fraser explained, "They couldn't navigate the grays."

"The grays," meaning "gray areas," separate the greats from role players. The ability to succeed and produce when working off-script is rare and indicative of immense confidence, combined with adroit facility. Harrison Barnes was a decent enough player, but he wasn't right for the grays. That was okay for the Warriors because, on the night they drafted Barnes, they would also take a man who could unlock power from the grays like he was unsheathing Excalibur out of stone. Unlike Barnes, he would not look the part

of a super athlete. At times, his physique seemed more bowling alley than basketball court. Unlike Barnes, he would curse at his opponents, yell at coaches, and party relentlessly. Unlike Barnes, he would be taken in the second round and be expected to do very little. Ultimately, he would have a huge hand in changing a sport few were sure he'd earn a place in.

"My favorite play is no play," Draymond Green once told me at a practice in 2016. The man thrived in chaos because he thought a bit faster than the rest. Sure Draymond could run whatever play was called, but he preferred to rely on his preternatural intuition. His instincts, especially his instincts on the defensive end, kept earning Green minutes. Eventually, he would have a legitimate claim as the second-best player on a seventy-three-win team.

After the successful 2012–2013 season in which the Warriors not only made the playoffs but upset the Denver Nuggets in Round 1, an activating piece was added to the puzzle. It was a trade that Myers had declared his "Mount Everest," a deal that had the normally well-put-together man looking unshaven and out of sorts at the press conference announcement of its completion.

Then Nuggets star Andre Iguodala was intrigued by what the Warriors were and believed he could improve it. Rob Pelinka, Iguodala's agent at the time, had a relationship with Myers from back when they worked together. This gave Myers an in, in addition to a plan. The goal was to acquire Iguodala's services while ceding little of on-court value.

"For many days and nights it was on life support," Myers said afterward. "I'd say to [my wife], the worst thing is, we spend so many hours on this and it's just not going to get it done."

In order to create the salary cap space, Myers tirelessly worked the phones, searching for a team that might take on expiring contracts. Finally, the Utah Jazz agreed to take the Warriors' junk,

accepting the contracts of Andris Biedrins, Brandon Rush, and Richard Jefferson. There was a cost associated, of course. The Warriors would have to give away draft picks.

The deal with the Jazz may have had elements of crafty arbitrage. Two of the picks the Warriors traded away were unprotected first-rounders (2014, 2017), something teams are loath to part with. The Warriors gambled that they'd stay out of the lottery and relied on the allure of "unprotected" to close the deal. When I initially wrote up how this deal happened in an article, I elided some of the finer details of salary dumping. A week after the article published, Myers grabbed my shoulder in the locker room tunnel and made sure to remind me. This deal had sapped much of his life force. He at least wanted every element of it honored in print.

Myers's efforts were not in vain. The Warriors had quickly, faster than anyone could have reasonably expected, built a roster that would go on to storm the league. Lacob and company had inherited Steph Curry. Within a roughly two-year span, the surrounding core of Thompson, Green, and Iguodala was added, plus Andrew Bogut and Shaun Livingston as important supplementary pieces.

That team would unleash a defensive revolution upon the NBA, concurrent with Steph Curry's activation of a game-warping offense from beyond deep range. The latter revolution got more headlines; the former changed the league more radically. The Warriors blitzed the NBA with a defense founded on versatility. They used wing-sized players (guys in the six foot six range) at most positions, and often slid wing-sized Draymond into the center spot. Draymond at center, flanked by Barnes, Iguodala, Thompson, and Curry came to be known as "the Death Lineup," a term coined by the writer Vincent Goodwill to describe a unit that ran up the score on plodding foes.

In this look, undersized Draymond exposed opposing centers, shutting them down on one end and racing past them on the other. Draymond's play was influential, as other teams began to copy the small ball look in a phenomenon that would eventually, completely invert the NBA's salary structure. Green himself spoke to the phenomenon when he got into a Twitter spat with then Heat center Hassan Whiteside. On August 26, 2015, Whiteside tweeted, "Small ball only works on centers that can't score #factsonly I wish you would put Someone that 6'6 on me #careerhigh#highschooldays." Draymond tweeted back, "Can you score doe? Bigs becoming dinosaurs." Whiteside would ink a $98 million deal that off season with the old-school Miami Heat, after which he would score with worse efficiency in each of the following four seasons.

Before Draymond and company upended the league, big men were paid handsomely to be, among other things, defensive anchors. Indeed, this is why the Warriors made their trade for Andrew Bogut early in Myers's reign. Wing defense wasn't as highly prioritized. It was too abstract, too difficult to measure. The Warriors believed they had a method for gauging its value and so they kept stocking up on perimeter defensive players in the six foot six to six foot eight height range. By 2014, the Warriors had Draymond Green, Andre Iguodala, Klay Thompson, Harrison Barnes, Shaun Livingston, and Justin Holiday, all on the same roster.

In another era, this collection of defenders might not have made such an impact. In the 1990s, when the NBA had "illegal defense" rules that legislated pockets of space for big men in the low post, such collective talent might have been squandered. This was a new era, however, one in which teams kept adding more and more three-point shooters. The entire perimeter was becoming a danger zone. In this environment, the Warriors seized upon a market inefficiency.

"It doesn't just happen," then assistant GM Travis Schlenk told me in 2015 of the Warriors loading up on defensive wings. "When you look at the guys, other than Andre [Iguodala] and Shaun [Livingston], they're all guys we've drafted. We've made a focal point from when I came on the front office side. The guys we've looked to draft have all been long."

Assistant coach Ron Adams, who started his coaching career during the Lyndon B. Johnson administration, was hired to head coach Steve Kerr's staff as a kind of experienced sage. Adams was known as a defensive guru, and unlike the stereotypical senior citizen, he was open to experimentation. In the second round of the playoffs in his first Warriors season, Adams would change the league with one seemingly wacky choice. The Grizzlies had led the Warriors 2–1 in the series, thanks in part to defensive ace Tony Allen causing chaos in Golden State's offensive schemes. Adams suggested that the Warriors defend Allen, a shooting guard who couldn't shoot, with Andrew Bogut merely watching him from the paint. The Warriors tried this in Game 4, inspiring awful misses from Allen as the Grizzlies offense gummed up. The series ended in short order. Other teams took note and started targeting non-shooters like the Sixers' Ben Simmons with similar strategies in playoff situations. It's now open season on non-shooters, like never before. Because of that, these Adams-style schemes have had major implications on roster and salary allocation.

To Adams, the strategy quirk was obvious if not boring. He had seen it all in his five decades. Adams had coached for so long, in so many places, that the lines between old and new blurred. He could conjure a trend out of what worked for his college squad in the 1960s.

Early in the training camp of 2014, Adams remarked, "You know, I think we could be a really good 'red' team." In the NBA, defense tends to be color coded, though the colors mean different

things on different squads. To Adams, "red" meant "switch." Switching, the practice of defenders trading assignments when one of them gets screened, was viewed with deep suspicion by basketball traditionalists, even if it worked for Adams back at Fresno Pacific. There was an element of machismo to this. To "switch" means to give up on the initial assignment, to abandon the challenge of guarding your man. It could also just look plain unnatural. Suddenly you see a point guard defending a center or vice versa. It can appear like a willfully chosen disaster.

In a 2005 *Inside the NBA* segment, Charles Barkley, with support from cohost Kenny Smith, ripped the Dallas Mavericks for switching on occasion. "I think that any team that switches every pick and roll, it always creates mismatches and destroys your defense," Chuck said. "That means they're not a good defensive team."

Mavericks owner Mark Cuban defended his team on his blog and said the stats validated the practice. This had been true for years. While switching was distrusted and avoided by traditionalists, stats tended to favor the approach over other methods that conceded space en route to a recovered assignment.

Roughly a decade later, what made the Warriors different was just how tailored their roster was to this long-resisted practice. So many of their defenders were of a similar size. I noted that in my 2015 article on the defense's rise: "The interchangeability of the resistance flusters offenses. Screen Iguodala, and here comes Thompson, who happens to be the exact same height. Screen Thompson, and here comes Green, who happens to be the exact same height. Golden State's defense is like the T-1000 Terminator villain who casually regenerates whatever body parts you blast off his corpus."

Draymond Green was key to the defense's dominance, as he could switch any assignment, 1 through 5, point guard through center. His ability to guard everyone was unusual and essential.

He fell in the draft because nobody was quite sure of his position. From the same article: "Draftniks and teams didn't quite know what to make of a guy standing 6-foot-5.75 in socks, with regular-person body fat, who rarely created his own shot. He was a classic 'tweener,' stuck somewhere between a big man and a guard—except he's somehow learned enough to transition from in-between to a one-size-fits-all. It's a rare player who can swipe Chris Paul and swat Dirk Nowitzki."

Of course, if Draymond Green was essential in vaulting the Warriors to new heights, what does it say about the "Light-Years" theory that he went thirty-fifth in the draft? The Warriors effectively passed on him twice, choosing worse players each time. The Warriors would counter that they deserve credit for working Draymond out and seeing his potential. Other teams could have gotten Green. It wasn't just a coincidence that he wound up in Oakland.

In truth, nobody within the Warriors saw Steph Curry's career coming either. Nobody at Warriors HQ likes to admit it, but many a GM knows: Curry was shopped around a lot before he became *Steph Curry*. Does that reflect poorly on the organization? Not necessarily. Curry appeared to have chronic ankle issues and struggled to stay on the court when under the care of the old Tom Abdenour medical staff.

Still, it shows that the Warriors weren't psychic. You can be ahead of the curve, maybe even light-years ahead, without knowing the future. In one prospective move that would have radically altered the NBA, the Warriors attempted to trade Steph Curry *and* Klay Thompson for Chris Paul in 2011. It was far from the only time Curry was shopped, but in this instance, the deal got fairly close to completion. Myers made the offer and Hornets GM Dell Demps was receptive. The catch was Chris Paul, who wanted out of New Orleans but had no intention of playing for the woebegone

Warriors. Paul told the Warriors they could do this trade, but he wouldn't be staying when his contract was up at season's end. With that, the Hornets lost out on the greatest backcourt of all time. Instead, in exchange for Paul, the Hornets would receive Eric Gordon, center Chris Kaman, Al-Farouq Aminu, and a draft pick that became Austin Rivers. A bit of a downgrade, somewhat mitigated by their winning the Anthony Davis lottery that offseason.

The Hornets weren't the only organization to narrowly lose out on the deal of a lifetime. According to one GM, "The Warriors were blind lucky that they were unsuccessful in trading Steph and Klay together for the stars they offered them together for," he said. "There were many, many people they tried to get and failed."

A notable road fork happened in 2012, in the beginning stages of the Warriors trading for Bogut. A Curry deal was discussed in a process that got far enough along to where his medical documents were sent to Milwaukee. Those documents were red-flagged by the Bucks' medical staff and not without reason. The Bucks staff determined what indeed proved so: Curry would require an ankle surgery, which he ended up undergoing in April. The surgery was successful enough for Curry to reclaim his career. Coming off the procedure, Curry would agree to a four-year, $44 million extension that offseason. While that's quite a bit of money for most people, it would prove to be a historically awesome bargain for a player who'd go on to win two MVPs.

At his 2015 executive of the year award ceremony, Bob Myers fielded a question on taking a big risk that paid off. Warriors players had filtered into the ceremony, down from their practice court a few floors above. Curry was slumped against the ballroom's back wall, wearing sweats and sandals, taking in the speech. In response to the big risk question, Myers cited the Curry extension, given all the doubts surrounding Curry's health and trajectory. History, in all its creeping determinism, did not view signing Steph as this

ballsy play. Nobody was quick to credit the Warriors for making the right choice. In the middle of Myers's explanation, Steph got up, pushed the double doors open, and left.

Were the Curry near trades grievous missteps? Did the Warriors ever really know what they were doing? One perspective is that the Warriors were lucky that they failed in acting on their wants. The internal perspective is that they still would have made success happen somehow, some way, if certain outcomes changed. Lacob, a devoted blackjack and poker player, somehow believes in probability simultaneously with believing in the power of belief. If the Warriors cleaned up their organization, they stood to shift the decision-making odds in their favor. If they embraced the wisdom of an informed crowd, its collective, engaged intelligence would prevail.

The Warriors can point to one near miss in particular as evidence of their process winning out. Famously, in the summer of 2014, after much deliberation, the Warriors nearly traded Klay Thompson for Kevin Love. The Minnesota Timberwolves were looking to unload a disgruntled All-Star and the Warriors, it was assumed by almost all league observers, did not have enough star power for a championship run. At that point in his career, Klay had shown flashes of what he later became, but not with high-level efficiency. In contrast, Love had just submitted a season in Minnesota that drew MVP buzz.

Jerry West was a highly pro-Thompson voice in the proceedings, as was the newly hired Steve Kerr. West was convinced that the offense run by Mark Jackson—the team's head coach for Thompson's whole career at that point—had hindered his production. Under Jackson, the Warriors were averaging the fewest passes of any team, and Thompson was a player who thrived off receiving passes on the move. Despite not being a modern analytics maven, old Jerry West intuitively grasped that more passing would help a

shooter dependent on rhythm. History would prove West correct, and history did not hesitate. Klay became a star that season, and the Warriors won their first championship in forty years.

Is there a lesson in the Klay Thompson almost-trade? One in particular might be the following theory: Teams really don't know what they have until they have the right coach. If a coach isn't optimizing talent, massive talent evaluation mistakes can occur, the kinds that cost franchises tens of millions in misallocated salary.

In this instance, Jackson's firing validated Lacob's hands-on approach to ownership. "Joe is very involved in the day-to-day stuff that we do, which is good," Warriors assistant GM Larry Harris said over the phone. "He's very engaged." On draft night, Joe is in the war room, invested alongside his Ops hires. The Golden State Warriors are not a lavish side project for him.

Not all in Ops like to admit it, but you usually need pressure from the top. An absence of it creates a power vacuum and power vacuums lead to destabilizing power struggles. This was the state of the Warriors under former owner Chris Cohan. At various times, nobody knew where the power resided, and constant chaos ensued. At one point, then president Bobby Rowell was working around then GM Chris Mullin and negotiating ill-advised deals, like a needless three-year extension for Stephen Jackson when Jackson still had two years left on his contract. Marcus Thompson, then a reporter for the Bay Area News Group, tells a story from the days leading up to that contract signing. Jackson was engaged in conversation with Thompson until he spied Rowell across the room. "Hold on," Jackson said. "Let me let this motherfucker think I like him so I can get this money." Jackson would get his money and demand a trade that very same season. This is what happens under absentee ownership.

There is, of course, a balance to be aspired to. You wouldn't want too antsy an owner, the kind who makes hasty choices based

off the last thing he read in the newspaper. The Suns' Robert Sarver has that reputation, but he's far from alone. Too much thin-skinned meddling is indeed a problem.

Joe might not have been a meddler on the level of other owners, though he was highly involved. Why? Well, he appeared to have fewer actionable opinions than other owners. "The Lacobs never give their opinions on players," a Warriors employee once told me, with a sigh. In the Basketball Ops world, this can be seen as a flaw, an indictment of someone who never puts skin in the game. In the Ops world, if you go all in on a player who busts, you wear that failure. It gets you fired. These takes aren't just takes. There's no parlaying them into entertainment fodder in the way Colin Cowherd does his "Colin was wrong" radio segment. These are grievous errors, lingering markers of one's unreliability. Yet the Lacobs, even though they had all the power, didn't even risk much reputation.

That was one read on their absence of opinions. There's another, more charitable perspective. There might be a methodology to asking instead of telling. Larry Harris said, "Sometimes the best advice is listening. Joe's really good at that. People can make all kinds of assumptions on what kind of owner he is, 'Light-Years,' and what not. Joe Lacob's best skill as an owner, and he's never had to do it because he owns the team, is he listens. He actually listens to what we have to say. It's not, 'I already know, and I'll just let you guys talk and you just do what I say.' It's never been that way."

Joe Lacob, for all his brashness, prides himself on "doing our homework, VC style." That means canvassing as many opinions as possible. This is how many Warriors decisions went down time and time again, according to Harris. "We talk and we talk and Joe goes 'Guys, I just want to hear this, would you do it or not? I just want to hear what you guys have to say.' We all say what we have

to say, and he goes 'You know what? We have a consensus. I agree with what you guys are saying. It makes sense. Let's go with it.'"

Such canvassing isn't without pressure, or even mind games. One of the franchise's foundational moves occurred shortly after Lacob took over, when flashy guard Monta Ellis was traded to the Milwaukee Bucks for burly defensive center Andrew Bogut. Warriors Basketball Ops had been working after this end for some time. Ellis wasn't a popular figure within the organization; he was thought to be an asshole. More importantly, he was thought to be too small and defensively suspect to continue on in that backcourt setup. Ellis himself famously admitted as much, declaring on media day of 2009, "You can't put two small guys out there . . . when you've got big two guards in the league."

Of the trade, Kirk Lacob recalled, "Over the course of this week, there was a lot of [Joe Lacob] positioning us to have a voice on the matter, and trusting the people who he had hired to do their jobs. Then what he really wanted to know at the end was, 'Okay, brought you all here to do this thing, we're doing this thing, now how strongly do you believe in it?' Or are you just going to let it happen? Because there's a difference between helping someone cross the finish line, and kind of letting it just happen."

With the deal nearly done, Joe Lacob entered the war room, and announced an inconvenient opinion. Kirk Lacob recounted, "He walks in, he goes, 'Hey, I don't want to do this.'" The room, including Bob Myers and then assistant GMs Larry Harris, Travis Schlenk, and Larry Riley, fought back and argued for the trade anew. Joe was testing their commitment to the choice. The Warriors would end up going through with the deal, a trade unpopular enough to get Joe Lacob roundly booed at GM Chris Mullin's retirement ceremony. Despite the initial backlash, it would prove to be a trade that helped the Warriors improve their defense and unleash Steph Curry's talents on offense.

Collective decision-making might be the savviest process, but it happens to rely on the strength of the team making the decisions. However, after the Warriors built up their juggernaut, theoretically important aspects of the franchise started disappearing. "With Joe, everyone has a price," said an employee who left the organization.

June 2017 provided evidence of this doctrine, when Jerry West left the Warriors after six years with the team. He had been a signature hire back in 2011, in the early days of Lacob and Guber's ownership, and a fixture at the top of the organization. But he decided to leave the Warriors over having been told to take a pay cut. "You have to be wanted," West said to Marc Stein of the *New York Times*. "Leaving the Warriors was probably the most difficult thing for me in my whole life. I didn't want to leave. You get to the point where maybe you don't feel as valued, but it's just something that happened. I hold no malice toward anyone over there."

West was maybe the most high-profile departure, but there were other notable ones. Sammy Gelfand, a well-regarded manager of analytics, left for the Detroit Pistons in the 2018 offseason. Performance therapist Chelsea Lane, also well regarded, left for the Atlanta Hawks that same offseason. The Hawks, which had drawn the aforementioned Travis Schlenk, Lane, Dan Martinez, and other ex-Warriors staffers, had earned the nickname "Warriors South." Lacob had a reputation for being stingy with staff salaries in the world's most expensive spot. In Atlanta, one's money spent so much better.

Did these departures matter? Or did Joe Lacob possess some kind of magic touch when it came to finding replacements? Perhaps these positions were ancillary after the main roster parts were secured and the right coach was found.

Getting to the point of "right coach" was a turbulent journey. Mark Jackson was hired on June 6, 2011, in a move of still debated

efficacy. Some would say Lacob, who was wowed in the interview
by Jackson's charisma, erred in the hire. While Lacob loved that
Jackson—who operated as a minister of his own Van Nuys, California, church—had a preacher's flair, he did not end up enjoying
all that came along with that. Jackson insisted on remaining a Los
Angeles–area pastor even while he coached in Oakland. To be a
pastor is to be integrated into a community in a way that makes it
difficult to leave. You have deep roots and ongoing issues to solve.

The Warriors weren't exactly ready for their coach to see the
Warriors as one of two full-time jobs. It was hard for Joe Lacob,
secular Jewish libertarian, to envision a religious commitment important enough to take hours and time away from one's vocation.

Just as importantly, Lacob also wasn't ready for Jackson's tendency to cordon the team off from Basketball Ops and the business side. That outcome ultimately proved fatal to Jackson's head
coaching tenure.

Though Steph Curry became a superstar under Jackson and
the Warriors made the playoffs, the end of Jackson's run was cha-
otic. He was not open to the hiring of better assistants, preferring
to employ men who would never threaten his status as HC. Assistant coach Brian Scalabrine was effectively fired in front of other
staffers with eleven games remaining in the season. A few weeks
later, assistant coach Darren Erman was fired for attempting to
record what he felt was an undermining effort from Jackson's favored assistants. One of those assistants, Lindsey Hunter, would
go on to threaten yours truly at a playoff practice, snarling that he
wanted to see me on the street and fight me. I'd written an article
that noted the lack of a winning record among the remaining assistants and had apparently struck a nerve. Suffice it to say, this
was a disordered time for the team.

Though the franchise rose under Jackson's stewardship, it was
easy to conclude that a lot of talent wasn't being optimized during

that run. Many still believe that Jackson was a good coach for a young team and that the team grew under his tutelage. Jackson got the team from point D to point B. There is a philosophy on coaches within the NBA. They aren't necessarily broken down according to a binary "good" versus "bad." Certain coaches are believed to be adept at moving a young team in the right direction, but not necessarily doing any better than that. They can raise a team's ceiling, but at a certain point, they become that team's ceiling. Lacob and company would probably deem Jackson one of those coaches.

Some see that theory as overly complicated, believing in the "good" versus "bad" coach binary. Andrew Bogut once said of Jackson's forty-seven-win season, "A literal dog could have coached us to forty-seven wins." In the offseason of 2014, after the Mark Jackson–led team had lost a seven-game series to the Clippers, the Warriors fired their coach.

It's difficult to see the Warriors as prescient on the coaching front, and not just because the Jackson era was so tumultuous. It's also because, after Jackson was canned, Lacob and company attempted to woo former Magic coach Stan Van Gundy, who had demonstrated a facility with deploying a three-point heavy attack.

In the end, their entreaties were outdone by the Detroit Pistons, who gave Van Gundy a dual role as coach and general manager, tantalizing if not corrupting power for a man who'd once been run out of town by his superstar player, back in Orlando. In retrospect, the Van Gundy hire would have likely been a mistake for the Warriors. Mark Jackson was a player's coach who favored light practices and maintained locker room unity by casting himself as the players' lone ally against the invidious motives of management. Van Gundy was detail-oriented and notoriously tough on players. "Teams, they always overcorrect," coaching agent Warren LeGarie once told me of team hiring practices. "It's human psychology. You go for the opposite of the coach you just

fired and maybe you go too far." Going from one to the other indeed might have been an adjustment, to say the least.

Instead, the Warriors hired a more relaxed kind of coach, a Southern California scion of academics. He was a man with enough status and money to eschew saving face in favor of giving it. That opened up possibilities for the Warriors. At a December 2014 luncheon for venture capitalists, Lacob said of his new hire, "I think he will be great. And he did the one big thing that I wanted more than anything else from Mark Jackson [that] he just wouldn't do, in all honesty, which is hire the very best."

Lacob continued, "Carte blanche. Take my wallet. Do whatever it is to get the best assistants there are in the world. Period. End of story. Don't want to hear it. And [Jackson's] answer . . . was, 'Well, I have the best staff.' No you don't. And so with Steve, very, very different."

Steve Kerr indeed was very different. Jackson had pumped up his younger players with public praise, but his reign was, in many ways, defined by internal insecurity. His assistant coaches weren't allowed to talk to media. This is a fairly common NBA practice, but in this instance, assistants were warned against getting too much shine. His refusal to accept supplementary help was a last straw of sorts, rooted in fear. The team's demise was a lesson in how destabilizing insecurity can be to group dynamics. It's an undermining, atomizing force, especially in the realm of management.

Kerr not only allowed Lacob to sign top-level assistants like Alvin Gentry and the aforementioned Adams, but Kerr was unusually deferential to them, seeking out their ideas and crediting their specific suggestions in the media. In general, Kerr was obsessed with the minds of coaches from all walks of life, in all sports. This had something to do with why, when Steve Kerr arrived in Oakland, ready to make his mark on the league, he had football on the brain.

3

THE INVENTION OF KERR

THE KERR ERA BROUGHT GREAT SUCCESS, ALL THE WHILE promoting the idea that success could actually be enjoyed. It was an intoxicating message in Rat Race America. Ultimately, that message could not be sustained under the weight of all its coinciding accomplishments.

When I spoke with Steve Kerr, he was down in San Diego on a brief respite, walking Luna, his beloved golden-chow mix. It's the time of year where Kerr seeks to "fill up his cup," as he says. That's part of his philosophy, borrowed from his former coach and mentor, Greg Popovich: the grind is impossible without occasional absence from it. The 2019 offseason was shorter than most, due to Kerr's Team USA basketball commitment in August. He opted to avoid Summer League this time around. "It's kind of become a jobs fair," he lamented of all the prospective scouts and coaches angling for a gig under the pretext of making conversation.

No doubt there are many coaches and leading NBA people who get approached this way during the offseason, Kerr especially has many aspirational greeters. He seems more approachable than

the standard coach, based on an affable public persona and years spent as a national broadcaster. Strangers feel like they know him, which can have its downsides. When you're out in public with Kerr, hardly a moment passes before someone asks for a selfie.

Once, when I was walking with him through the lobby of the Mandalay Bay, a would-be photo taker walked right past Sixers coach Brett Brown and, toddler in hand, approached Kerr. As the young boy cried, his father said to Kerr, "He really wants a photo with you." "I can see that," Kerr said, in a tone that was somehow sarcastic without being biting. He shrugged and apologized his way out of the uncomfortable interaction.

"I hate that," Kerr said after the selfie-seeking father left. "It's just messed up when people use their kids to get a selfie when you can clearly tell the kid doesn't give a shit."

Apparently this happens to celebrities. Though fame offers incredible benefits and experiences, such status also has a certain way of exposing our culture's VIPs to the ugliness in humans. You constantly see people use their children as emotional blackmail.

Kerr can cynically comment on this, and be reliably mordant about so many current events. In another moment, he will come off as a true believer, a nouveau hippie in touch with basketball's more spiritual side. Kerr extols the virtues of "playing with joy." As with his former coach Phil Jackson, abstract conceptions came with plenty of concrete accomplishments. His arrival in Oakland in the summer of 2014 instantly coincided with the gear-shift into greatness. He took a talented, low- to mid-tier playoff team and it turned into an unexpected champion. Then, the following season, that team broke the all-time record for single season wins with seventy-three.

Something happened in the summer of 2014 and kept going. It was clear that the Warriors implemented and integrated a philosophy that has served them. Kerr is inclined to deflect credit, but

he'll talk about coaching philosophy. "[Gregg Popovich] tells me I share too much," Kerr said of his fairly open media sessions. "He texts me when I give something away in a press conference. But he comes from the military and I'm the child of academics." And so we got into the origins of playing with joy.

"I saw Tom Friedman the other day," he said of meeting with *The World Is Flat* author and *New York Times* columnist. "I asked him about the lack of White House press briefings." This seemed like a non sequitur, perhaps a current events–inspired digression into the errors of a president Kerr isn't too fond of. But indeed, the story was going somewhere.

"I expected Friedman to answer with the reason of it's important that the American people deserve to know what's going on. Right? That's obviously the answer, right?"

That wasn't the real answer, or the complete one anyway, in the columnist's estimation.

"Friedman told me, 'Ya that's important, but what's really important is that the administration, when they are forced to present something to the American people every day, in effect, what it forces them to do is create a policy and create a vision and create a philosophy. Instead, they've basically cut out all communication. So they have no philosophy, they have no policy. When they need to refer to a policy, they reverse engineer it. Whereas, in the beginning, if they had press briefings they would've been forced to form some thoughts.'

"I thought that was fascinating," Kerr said with a laugh.

If Joe Lacob believes in the power of speaking great feats into existence, Steve Kerr believes in the power of writing thoughts into existence. Lacob boasts his dreams into reality, and Steve Kerr writes them into implementation. Kerr workshopped his thoughts until they formed a philosophy. Then and only then did he feel ready to hold a clipboard.

Kerr had always wanted to be a coach, even more so than wanting to be a player, but did not quite know how to begin. He was popular as a TNT announcer, which gave him an in with the owners. None may admit it but many owners prefer to hire coaches off the television. Chalk it up to an "I see it, I want it" rich guy mentality. Incidentally, Mark Jackson was working as an ESPN announcer when Joe Lacob gave him cash and clipboard.

So Kerr had options, far better options than the standard rookie coach. He would be able to start at the top in a field full of envious assistants, grinders who would never rise close to the postgame podium. That was a blessing, but being fast-tracked comes with concerns. Preparation would have to be key to offset the pratfalls of inexperience. In Basketball Ops, people are usually oriented toward demonstrating what they know rather than exposing themselves to the vulnerability of asking. Kerr prefers the latter approach.

"I told Jeff Van Gundy I wanted to coach and I asked him his advice," Kerr recalled. "He said, 'Write down everything that comes to mind and keep it in a file and organize it and develop a philosophy. Do it on your own time and as you think of stuff, just pull out your computer and type away and maybe put it away for a week, and you do it again the next week.'"

Coaches don't just draw up plays and make substitutions. They teach. I sometimes ask up-and-comers in Basketball Ops why they aspire to be a GM, as many of them do. Most struggle with the question and can't manage to espouse more than a belief that they'd do it well. The goal was always there, but like our common want to exist, the reasons for why are less clear. Coaches usually have better answers for why they want to coach and what they seek to accomplish with their coaching. This is an intellectual pursuit as much as it is a competition for money and status.

The preparation advice Kerr got from the late Flip Saunders was more amusingly general than thoughtful, though. "I worked with Flip at TNT, he did a few games with Marv and me years ago," Kerr said. "I asked him the same question and he said, 'Just make sure when you sit down with an owner, you bring a lot of stuff.' And I said, 'Well, what do you mean a lot of stuff?' He goes, 'I don't know. It could just be a binder of a bunch of plays, but the main thing with owners was to have them look at a bunch of stuff because then they think you've really really put a lot of time into it.'"

Kerr had his marching orders. He needed to come up with a coaching philosophy and put it into the form of "a lot of stuff." He tinkered with his "manifesto," slowly adding and adding until it turned into thirty pages. "It covered everything from travel policies, like who's allowed on the plane, who's not, to what our office would look like, to do we have a cell phone policy and the locker room, to what happens if a guy doesn't play, is he required to get a workout in that night after the game? I mean, anything I could think of, I had that in there. And then, once I knew I was interviewing with the Warriors, I really added to it and catered to their roster and added a few pages of things that I thought philosophically that I would do, either the same or differently, and kind of tweak whatever and we talked about all that stuff."

It was good to write all of this down, and it all looked impressive when Kerr pitched the Warriors brain trust in Oklahoma City, while there to announce playoff games. Lacob had already succeeded with a neophyte GM in Bob Myers. Though the Warriors swung and missed on Stan Van Gundy, they were sufficiently impressed with Kerr's overall vision and vision for their team specifically.

Kerr got the job but he needed more. Something was missing. He had plans but he still lacked a philosophy. He believed the latter to be important, important enough that he went in search of it.

"The guy who negotiated my contract with the Warriors was Mike Tannenbaum, who was the GM of the Jets couple of years prior to that," Kerr said. "After Mike negotiated my contract, he told me, 'All right, now it's time to get to work.' And I said, 'What do you mean?' He said, 'You got to get ready for training camp. Let's get you with as many coaches as possible and sit down and pick their brains and really think about how you're going to coach the Warriors.'"

In Tannenbaum's world, "coaches" meant NFL coaches. Kerr, who was a big football fan, was going to draw off the NFL for an NBA intellectual foundation. It was just crazy enough to work. First, Tannenbaum set up a meeting with a man whose acerbic, East Coast tough guy persona seemed superficially at odds with anything affable SoCal Steve might emulate in the NBA. Nevertheless, Kerr did a detour on the way to visiting family in upstate New York, just to meet Bill Parcells.

"I stopped at Saratoga Country Club and had lunch with Bill and asked him about coaching," Kerr said. "It was fascinating. And, needless to say, Bill and I couldn't be more different from one another but it was awesome. It was awesome hearing him talk about how to reach players."

Coaches rarely speak publicly about an obvious aspect of the job they perhaps dwell on most of all: how to communicate with the young millionaires in their midst. To speak about it openly might ruin the effect of what's being attempted, like telling the patient that he's taking a placebo. Also, it's dangerously close to claiming public credit, which can fuel certain resentments.

This communication is not as intuitive a skill as one might think for these coaches. Sure, everyone in sports is a jock and speaks a certain lingo, but there are divisions and tensions within. Early on, I used to think I was awkward when talking to players because I'm a white nerd, not to mention a member of

the media (in the players' universe, this essentially makes me a hall monitor). While that might well be so, the first few times I was privy to an exchange between player and coach, usually in the form of a postgame locker room visit for the sake of communicating logistics, I was shocked at how much it mirrored the discomfort of my own interactions. It's easy to slap a guy's back after a game-winning shot and a whole lot harder to explain why you're suspending him for breaking a team rule or sending him down to the G League.

In the NBA, coaches meetings often spend large amounts of time on how to motivate an otherwise demoralized athlete. "How do we tell him he's coming off the bench?" is a standard problem. If the news is communicated poorly, you could "lose" the player to resentment, obstinacy, or diffidence, depending on personality. Coaches are not credited with how they maintain motivation or turn a player's season around, because how could anyone know from the outside? Still, it's a huge aspect of their jobs, if not the biggest.

"I remember that Bill told me that he liked to turn things back over to the player in a very forceful manner," Kerr said of an intriguing Parcells tactic.

"I said 'What do you mean?' And he said, 'Well, if a player's underperforming I'll bring him into my office and I'll say, 'Apparently I have more confidence in your ability to perform than you do.' And it was sort of a way to motivate/shame/anger, however you want to put it, and yet still maintain the upper hand. 'I just told you that I have more confidence in you than you do. So I have confidence in you.' So it's sort of an abstract way of saying, 'You're not getting the job done and it's your own fault.'"

The Parcells tactic is a way of expressing disappointment while reminding the player that he still has agency to thrive and survive. Critique absent demoralization is an art. This is the constant

tension in coaching and in many management positions. You must be a clear communicator, but also manipulative in a way.

"You've got to be honest, but if you just say it bluntly it might not get across," Kerr explained. "It might be offensive. One of the reasons I think players listen to me when I criticize them is because I tend to criticize myself first. I really coached a shitty game, but here's what we could have done differently."

This is standard Kerr, giver of face. It's not that Kerr lacks an ego. He might actually have enough of an ego, or at least enough self-confidence, to take shots at himself. Coming on as a rookie coach, he did not feel so emboldened to do it any other way. He did not feel like he had the cachet to regularly scream at his players in the manner Gregg Popovich does. "Pop" is famous for his humiliating tirades, or, as it's called in the Spurs' organization, "Going Serbian."

This is a difference in leadership style. Popovich has that quality we might call "smart-mean," a crotchety expression of intellect that connotes a certain intimidating gravitas. Kerr has to go another way. Or, to quote *The Onion* headline, "NBA Commentators Confirm Steve Kerr Not Enough of an Insufferable Prick to Be Considered All-Time Great Coach."

"First of all, he's more accomplished, so he has free rein to just goes nuts on his players if he wants," Kerr said when asked of the comparison. As a rookie coach, Kerr definitely felt a gravitas chasm between himself and some of the more established play callers like Popovich and Rick Carlisle. For one, they seemed more capable in intimidating referees, a suspicion that gnawed at him more than any sense that he had less leeway in screaming at players.

"I hadn't earned that right to go nuts on my players, but it's probably, also, less my style," Kerr said. "I do go nuts once in a while, as you know. Very rarely is it to a player. Sometimes it's to the referees, sometimes it's to our little circle of coaches during the

timeout where I shatter a clipboard or something, and I'm angry at the team, but I take it out on the coaches instead."

That deflection tactic doesn't always work in our modern tech panopticon. "I think I got busted saying, 'I'm so tired of Draymond's shit,'" Kerr said of the time cameras caught him complaining on the sideline in a loss to the Suns, and Twitter caught the exchange. It wasn't long before expert lip readers had the Internet buzzing. Kerr had to flag Draymond down afterward to fix an issue that never would have existed in the 1990s.

When he came on as coach, Kerr operated with a sensitivity to showing up his players. He didn't initially do much coaching of Curry. After all, Steph had seen his stock rise gloriously under Mark Jackson, and Kerr might come off as presumptuous if he barged in with a bunch of reforming ideas. Instead Kerr waited for an early season rough patch of high-turnover games before going over film and giving pointers. Reform needed a context. It couldn't just show up, right off the plane from San Diego.

In general, Kerr's motivation techniques are utilitarian. He's looking for whatever works. Draymond Green's college coach Tom Izzo told Kerr to coach Green hard, and so he did.

"I mean, I yelled at him a lot my rookie year. Sometimes I would do it on purpose just to get him going. I remember we had a game in New Orleans and he went out after, I think it was after a timeout or maybe it was the start of the second half, and they went on a quick 8–0 run, but he didn't have his shoe tied when he got out to start the second half. He was tying his shoe while the ball is in play and they go on an 8–0 run, and I call timeout, and start yelling at the team, and I had looked at Draymond. I said, 'Your damn shoe is not even tied. You're telling me you're ready to play when your shoe's not even tied?' And he got so pissed and he went back out like the Incredible Hulk and we went on a big run. So I figured out that that was a good way to handle Draymond, until it wasn't."

While Popovich, Jackson, Parcells, and others had valuable pointers on the coaching profession, none were Kerr's kindred spirit in terms of philosophy. Kerr would find that in a fellow sanguine West Coaster, Seahawks coach Pete Carroll.

"It was the final piece for my preparation to coach the Warriors," Kerr said of his journey to Seahawks training camp in 2014. "But it was a critical piece because Pete had been coaching for a long time, obviously, and had given all of the stuff so much thought. I was sitting down with Pete in his office for three straight days, discussing coaching philosophy, and he shared his story and his story was fascinating. He told me he coached the Jets and the Patriots and he had done fine but he got fired. And then he took a job with the Niners and he had a very low-level job with the Niners, kind of starting over again."

Carroll did not have an obvious path back up the NFL food chain, but he did have access to Bill Walsh, a consultant for the 49ers at the time. At the end of every day Carroll would go sit in Walsh's office and just talk about life and football, and that's when he was able to form his philosophy on coaching, sitting there with Walsh.

Walsh relayed a methodology to Carroll that would reshape his conception of coaching. "So Walsh's key was, at that point everybody's got core values, right?" Kerr said. "Most companies have core values. You go into any weight room at any university, any professional team and you see posters on the wall, only the strong survive, protect each other, what the mottos are, and the next part was the critical part. Walsh said, 'Everything that you do every day has to reflect those core values.

"Pete said when he took the USC job, in his mind, he had figured it out. He's like, 'Okay, now I understand what coaching is about.' And he went into USC with unbelievable energy and enthusiasm, but clarity in terms of how he wanted to go about his business and the culture that he wanted to form. And he went and

had one of the greatest eight- to ten-year runs in college football history. I grew up a UCLA fan and I hated USC, but I loved watching them play when Pete was coaching. I couldn't take my eyes off the screen and one of the reasons was the joy with which they played. And so, I thought about that all the time and I told Pete, I said, 'I want the Warriors to look like USC did.'"

While Kerr had the intuition that he wanted to play like USC, the actual emulation was another thing. At the very least, writing down that goal and formalizing the process made it seem more attainable.

"So I knew that that's kind of how I wanted to operate but what I had never really thought about was putting that down on paper. Like what does that mean? How do you achieve culture on paper? You don't do it on paper but you can describe it on paper and then work to achieve it based on the principles that you have thought about and formulated in your mind and in your gut. What Pete did was, he said, 'What's most important to you in your life?' And he said, 'Think of like whatever's important to you, family, discipline, anything that you think has been a guiding force for you. Think of it, write it down, and then we'll talk tomorrow. Come in and bring whatever you have tomorrow.'

"I said, 'All right.' So I did that and I came in with seven or eight things and he said, 'These are good.' And he goes, 'Yours are going to be different from mine and mine are going to be different from Bill Parcells, because these things have to reflect you. Your coaching has to reflect who you are.' And so what I would do now is let's whittle this down to four things. Four values that you hold most dear to yourself, that you think are the most important ways to describe yourself and that you hold truest in your life. And that's where joy, compassion, competitiveness, mindfulness came from."

Maybe it sounded too simple to be true, but here Kerr was at Seahawks practice, seeing slogans come to life. "Always compete"

was a central slogan of Carroll's, but more than a slogan, it was a constant at Seahawks practices.

"I witnessed it for three days," Kerr said. "It was so genuine and the players were having so much fun and they were competing like crazy. I flew back to the Bay just on fire just thinking, 'All right! This makes sense now.' Your values have to come alive in the way you operate. And so you can't just say, 'Hey guys, let's be really competitive and let's have a lot of joy.' Every day had to reflect that. So the joy comes from music, comes from funny videos, it comes from talking shit about each other, making each other laugh. It's about letting guys be themselves and practical jokes, but the competition comes from turning everything into a competition. Every shooting game has to be . . . a winner and loser. In general, people in the NBA love to compete. So you bring it out of them but you make sure you do all that stuff in practice and if it happens every day and it's reflected in a genuine manner with a staff that is authentic in its goals and its communication, and you've got a willing audience, which we did, now you can capture some magic. And that's what I felt happened that year."

In that year, the Warriors exploded onto the basketball scene, going from lower-tier playoff threat to dominant force. It was visible immediately, even in the preseason, where they outscored opponents by an average of 11 points. It was like watching men who'd previously been walking on their hands finally start using their feet. The offense went from plodding to high movement, with the ball whipping around all over the floor. Between Steph Curry's effervescent dominance and the freewheeling teamwork on display, one did not sound all that corny calling this joy incarnate.

When I sat next to advance scouts, tasked with studying the Warriors for opposing teams, they'd tell me it was their easiest night of the season. The Warriors ran the fewest plays and relied

instead on fast-paced improvisation. No other team played quite this way, perhaps because no other team could. It wasn't chaos so much as a synchronicity founded in intelligence. The Warriors, blessed with more savvy pass-oriented veterans than anyone else, with an attack opened up by two historically great shooters, could turn the court into a theater of the mind.

When the Warriors won the 2015 NBA Finals, it was the culmination of a vision and an ethos. It was a validation that winning, though it required hard work, did not have to be drudgery. It could be a triumphant process that ultimately ends in triumph. Kerr called winning his first title "the greatest night of my life." Such highs do not sustain.

In March 2019, Kerr was reading an article on the rise of the Milwaukee Bucks, an aesthetically enjoyable team that had pundits drawing parallels to the 2014–2015 Warriors. "I threw my phone," Kerr said of his reaction. Well, not literally. Maybe.

"I'm not sure if I actually threw my phone," Kerr said. "It might have come at the same time that one of our guys was putting us in a difficult spot." Kerr did not name the particular guy, but it's not hard to guess.

"But that's just part of it," he continued. "I think for us, and for me personally, my first year coaching we went on that thrill ride the entire season. So we were on the climb that whole first year and, let's face it, I jumped in when they had already been on the climb for a couple of years, but they were still on the rise and searching and it was my job to help them get better. It was pretty amazing that, as a coach that was my first year, to experience that kind of high. Even though I knew this doesn't last and it can't always feel like this, it did feel like it would last forever."

Nothing does. As economist Herbert Stein's famous law dictates, "If something cannot go on forever, it will stop." While that

law is self-evident, despite our temporary illusions, rarely in the NBA does basketball nirvana die of natural causes. Egos get in the way, often before Father Time arrives on the scene.

In the case of the Warriors dynasty, their central, terminal issue was simple: they got more from Kevin Durant's presence than he was getting from them. At least that's how he eventually felt about it, otherwise leaving for a suspect Brooklyn Nets situation would have made little sense. I asked Kerr about the time KD mocked Kerr's principle of "playing with joy" in a press conference, after a blowout loss to the Celtics.

"Yeah," Kerr started. "That's a tough one because we all kind of could see what was happening." While higher-level Basketball Ops types might have held out hope for a KD recruitment, the traveling staff knew for a while. KD was gone, but for a few months in which he would remain on the Warriors but get mired in his mind.

"This is one that's difficult to talk about," Kerr said. "That was a difficult time of the season for all of us, but especially for Kevin, and it didn't surprise me. You could tell he was feeling a lot of stress."

Durant might have taken shots at Kerr, but in the end, like many within the Warriors, there's more sympathy than enmity toward him. There's a respect if not fear of what KD was going through. There's less a sense that Durant killed the joy than that what happened was beyond everybody, even him.

Still, Kerr would wonder if there was a way to combat the modern onslaught on the psyche. Maybe, just maybe, if he could do it all over, the power of actualization might defeat certain demons.

"I have this idea to someday bring in a few of their detractors from Twitter," Kerr said of the Twitter trolls. "Like actually find them and bring them, set the fans in front of them. 'Kevin, this is Joe from Portola Valley. Joe said that you were a loser yesterday.

Now look at him. Look at him carefully. Do you really care what he thinks?'"

This time, by bringing what's written into reality, Kerr might reveal its falseness as opposed to its self-evident truth.

"The flip side is, Joe would be completely embarrassed," Kerr said of his plan. "He'd be like, 'I can't believe I wrote that. I'm so sorry. I'm an idiot. Can I have your autograph?'"

It's a novel idea, and classic, playful Kerr. But it's too late. KD left. Now that he's gone, it gives Kerr less talent and more on-court obstacles. But the philosophy that brought the team to its greatest heights remains essential.

"Well, I think joy is an integral part of not just winning, but just living," said Kerr. "We've been lucky, we've been in this sweet spot the last five years where we had a chance to win a championship every single year, and that's pretty rare. But my philosophy on joy won't change just because we have less of a chance of winning a championship next year. To me, it's an integral part of life, just of your daily routine, and so it's something that will always be part of my coaching philosophy. I mean, how could we not search for that, playing basketball for a living and this position that we're in? I would feel to blame if we couldn't find joy in our circumstances, just knowing what's going on around the world and how difficult most people have it, and we're playing basketball and getting paid a ton of money to do it. You better find joy or I'm not doing my job."

Kerr's joy, mocked as it was near of end of KD's time, was essential to Durant's recruitment. A few Warriors officials believe that KD was drawn to the Warriors in part by All-Star Weekend 2015, when Kerr was coach of the West squad. It was Kerr at peak cheerful insouciance, months before a botched back surgery brought constant pain. He was cracking jokes and having fun with the absurd proceedings. At one point, the Warriors coaches were

drinking beers in their locker room when a curious Durant poked his head in.

"So this is what you're about, huh?" KD said, with a smile. The coaches didn't deny it.

"I know that the way we went about our business was pretty unique," Kerr said of the beers. "Very different from OKC and San Antonio, much looser. Players are given a lot more autonomy. I think that might have appealed to Kevin. I think after that first year, I think a lot of people watched us play around the league and they liked our style and they saw the joy that was being displayed by our players and our fans and they saw the talent. They saw the way our guys played and they wanted to be a part of it and I think that's what attracted Kevin."

Durant was attracted to the Warriors not just because they were winners, but because they were charismatic, free-spirited winners. He liked the freedom, how victory could happen within a framework of cheap beer, usually bottles of Modelo and cans of Coors Light. In that first Warriors season, he'd guzzle Coors post-game, sometimes letting out an elongated booze belch before his interviews. With the Warriors, KD could kick back. He could be himself.

The Warriors were in the spotlight but seemed to require less pressure than the Thunder. Beyond that, they already had a super-star MVP with whom Durant could share the load. Such an alliance is powerful and nearly unbeatable. The forces of industry and ego also made it tenuous.

4

SNEAKER WARS

IN THEORY, STEPH CURRY AND KEVIN DURANT HAD POWERFUL market forces working against their alliance. They joined up anyway. One did it for the Warriors, in defiance to his business partners. The other did it for his own reasons, in a move that made more business sense for his company than for himself.

Following a December 2015 victory over the Celtics, then Cleveland Cavaliers superstar LeBron James took the typical postgame questions, until a query deviated from the norm. A reporter asked him about the sneaker brand Under Armour—or at least tried to. LeBron interrupted, saying, "Who? Who? Who is that?"

James ended the conversation by revealing that only one (sneaker) team is fit for his lips, saying, "I only know Nike. That's it. Lifetime."

James indeed has a lifetime contract with Nike worth more than $500 million, according to *USA Today*. He's changed NBA teams three times, but he's always been and always will be a Nike guy. If that reporter had been allowed another subversive

follow-up, perhaps this question would have yielded interesting results: "Who is your primary employer?"

"Your primary employer is who pays you the most money," ESPN's Bomani Jones said when I spoke to him about this particular exchange. Jones, a keen observer and commentator on modern sports culture, expounded on that point. "LeBron was Team Nike before he was a Cleveland Cavalier or a member of the Miami Heat or any of those things. We contextualize guys around the teams they play for because that's the relevant variable for the kind of work that we do."

It's perhaps more comforting to believe the team commands primary allegiance. Of course, when it comes to success on the court, what's good for the goose is good for the gander. Nike wins if LeBron's Lakers win. It just so happens that James still wears Nikes for his next team, should he ever decide to ditch Los Angeles. And James will still draw checks from Nike, long after he's done with the Lakers. He's "lifetime," after all.

To many a player and sneaker executive, basketball is the means and one's brand is the ultimate end. The sneaker business exists parallel to the basketball business, except not completely. Estimates peg total sneaker sales somewhere north of $20 billion annually, and rising. The total worth of NBA basketball is harder to gauge, but the $2.15 billion sale of the traditionally ignoble Los Angeles Clippers in 2014 speaks to its riches. Both basketball and basketball shoes are massive operations, deriving their dollars from the consumer's obsession with winners. More specifically, with cool winners. Football can be ugly and popular. Baseball can be slow and profitable. The NBA needs physical charisma, individuals with moves so graceful viewers ache to imitate them.

You can't be Michael Jordan, but you can rent a part of his life when you wear Jordans. For millions of people, that slice of happiness is worth the cost.

In spring of 2016, kids the nation over were renting a slice of Steph Curry, at the expense of LeBron's and Nike's business. Nike had ignored and overlooked Curry, who used to be on their payroll until 2013. When pitching him to remain with Nike, they botched the meeting with some unintentional foreshadowing.

The pitch meeting, according to Steph's father, Dell, who was present, kicked off with one Nike official accidentally addressing Stephen as "Steph-on," the moniker, of course, of Steve Urkel's alter ego in *Family Matters*. "I heard some people pronounce his name wrong before," said Dell Curry. "I wasn't surprised. I was surprised that I didn't get a correction."

It got worse from there. A PowerPoint slide featured Kevin Durant's name, presumably left on by accident, presumably residue from repurposed materials. "I stopped paying attention after that," Dell said. Though Dell resolved to "keep a poker face," throughout the entirety of the pitch, the decision to leave Nike was in the works.

In the meeting, according to Dell, there was never a strong indication that Steph would become a signature athlete with Nike. "They have certain tiers of athletes," Dell said. "They have Kobe, LeBron and Durant, who were their three main guys. If he signed back with them, we're on that second tier."

Corporations fixate on whatever built them up to success. Nike was made by Michael Jordan, a high-flying wing. Smallish, less than athletic point guards don't factor into this model. That's how Steph Curry, whose launches aren't leaps, snuck up on them. The reason he was ignored was also the reason he became popular. Children gravitated to the dominant player whose teammates once nicknamed him "Middle School" for his youthful appearance. He was simultaneously the underdog and overdog, a crusher of opponents who could literally crush him.

On March 3, 2016, at the height of Curry Mania, *Business Insider* relayed a note from Morgan Stanley analyst Jay Sole on

Under Armour's business prospects. In it, Curry's potential worth to the company was placed at more than $14 billion.

His note read, "UA's U.S. basketball shoe sales have increased over 350 percent YTD. Its Stephen Curry signature shoe business is already bigger than those of LeBron, Kobe and every other player except Michael Jordan. If Curry is the next Jordan, our call will likely be wrong." Wrong, as in, at that moment, Steph Curry had the potential to be even more valuable than a mere $14 billion.

In the end, Curry never got close to that mark. Maybe such a feat was beyond his capability; maybe he was just too small, not durable enough, to be a dominant playoff superstar year after year after year. We would never quite find out what Steph Curry could have been as a cultural figure had he remained the undisputed Number One option on his team for the duration of his prime. Instead, he went another way, sacrificing status and business for the sake of success.

The basketball sneaker industry is as volatile as sports itself. A corporation that invests big-time shoe deals in players is like being a nation that pegs its currency to another country that's in a perpetual state of revolution. It's a high-variance business because so many eggs are in so few baskets. Potential billions are tied up in the outcomes rendered by a human body. If the body breaks, the corporation fails. There's a fair argument that Michael Jordan was more influential in building Nike than even Steve Jobs was in building Apple. Many nations have smaller GDPs than what would have been squandered had Michael Jordan torn his knee off a Bill Laimbeer hip check in the 1980s. Injury didn't topple Steph's empire in such a definitive way, but it left it wobbly. His business prospects didn't truly change until he decided, soon afterward, to share the stage.

The ebb of Steph's brand started on April 16, 2016. In Golden State's opening playoff game against Houston, following that in-

credible seventy-three-win Warriors regular season, Curry hurt his right ankle on a routine play. It looked like a mere nuisance. He turned on a change of possession, and started to limp slightly. Nothing dramatic and surely, we all assumed in the moment, nothing that would matter much. Steph had been dominant in his twenty minutes of action, scoring 24 points with an assertive command we've perhaps not seen since. He still has fantastic games and certainly has moments. Today's Steph is great, but his artistry rarely recaptures total command, powered by a subtly athletic burst, of that gestalt aura of Steph's 2016 superstardom.

That minor injury led to two missed playoff games. Slightly ominous, but who could be that worried when he returned to action in Game 4? Steph had been so confident in his health that he'd neglected to bring dress clothes on the road to Houston, the NBA sartorial version of Hernán Cortés burning his own ships on the beaches of Veracruz. Cortés was lucky, though. His conquest path never ventured into the dangerous waters of a Donatas Motiejunas sweat slick.

Steph was not so lucky. Motiejunas, a less than nimble Lithuanian big man, accidentally clicked his heels midsprint and slid, mostly on his ass, a literal thirty feet. Oblivious to the deluge, Steph moved across the path of the Motiejunas slip 'n' slide and collapsed into a quasi split, spraining his MCL.

Unlike the ankle tweak a few days before, the slip and fall in Houston was a legitimately scary sight. Curry cried on the court, comforted by Draymond Green. In the second half, the Warriors redoubled their efforts and, absent their superstar, still overwhelmed the Rockets. I remember that evening quite well. It was a shock to witness the vulnerability of the previously invincible. Steph was slight, but he'd overcome so much that you could have been lulled into thinking this arc a fairy tale, absent the accidents that fell mere mortals.

After the game, backstage of the Toyota Center, Joe Lacob was talking up the waiting media scrum, a rare-if-ever sight. He was gregarious, projecting optimism about the team in spite of Steph's possibly dire circumstances. Lacob could be counterintuitive that way, putting up a buoyant front in the wake of disaster. His never-ending quest to speak success into existence came with an impulse to speak it louder when it seemed farthest away.

It's difficult to predict how NBA insiders will react to awful news. The night of Kevin Durant's torn Achilles in 2019 brought a loud kind of public mourning from the Warriors, with Bob Myers literally crying in a press conference. April 16, 2016, brought a different vibe. Curry sat on a folding chair by his visitor locker and bantered, despite the circumstances. The Warriors role players who had come through weren't happy about what happened, but weren't weighed down by it either. "You got to," said Shaun Livingston, who himself had once suffered a devastating knee injury. "With athletes, you have to have a 'next man up' mentality."

That was a different Warriors team, one with more veterans and more resolve. Athletes tend to be optimists, so they probably assumed an ability to hold the fort for as long as it took to get Curry back.

Backstage of the Toyota Center, Steph's camp wasn't so confident. Ralph Walker, Curry's sage bodyguard, grimaced and shook his head. He lamented how the allowance of a James Harden game winner had changed everything, how the Warriors nearly swept the Rockets and earned their superstar some needed rest. "We were so close," Ralph muttered. He then excused himself to join Steph and a local pastor in a prayer circle. As Steph bowed his head in the huddle and prayed for medial collateral salvation, he gripped an oversized bag of popcorn, slung over the pastor's shoulder. Postgame popcorn on the road is a must for Steph. There certainly have been worse amulets.

Prayers were answered, as Steph indeed fought his way back that postseason, even willing himself to an incredible 40-point performance in his return game. But the almighty had granted only so much. In June, the Warriors famously lost a 3–1 Finals lead, Steph was ejected in Game 6, his wife floated ref conspiracy theories on Twitter, and worst of all, from Under Armour's perspective, his sneakers got roundly mocked on social media.

"Roundly mocked" likely understates the degree of shoe shaming. His sneakers became an object of ridicule in a manner that was simply unprecedented in the industry.

The Chef Curry 2s were a specific model, a "colorway" of the Curry 2 sneaker. For you sneaker novices, one of the cost-effective methods shoe companies use to gin up demand is by continually putting a new gloss on an old product. Every season brings a new sneaker, and that sneaker is given different colorways to excite and appeal to as broad a base as possible. Through something of a reverse alchemy, the all-white paint job of the Chef Curry colorway turned the model into undesirably archaic clogs.

They were deemed dad shoes. Jimmy Kimmel showed a whole comedy sketch based on the dad shoe premise. Stephen Colbert quipped, "Steph, these shoes look like a golf cart had sex with a jar of mayonnaise."

Russ Bengtson, a veteran sneaker industry journalist and fan of the Chef Curry model, pushed back against the phenomenon, saying, "Can you bully a shoe? Is that possible? Because that's what it felt like. It felt like high school, in the worst possible sense." Bengtson perhaps was right, but right matters little when it comes to what's cool. The morning after the Chef Currys went negatively viral, I ran into Under Armour executive Kris Stone at Pour coffee shop in Cleveland. I naively floated the idea that this could all be good for Under Armour. Kris, unshaven and visibly shaken after

a long night of brand emergency, was not so convinced. "This was not a good night," he said flatly.

Had Curry been averaging 40 points in the Finals, the social media pile-on would have been mitigated. Michael Jordan's "Flu Game" sneakers have the look of a mouth slathered in drunkenly applied red lipstick, and they're among his most beloved models. I'm convinced that the shoes don't make the man so much as the man makes the shoes. Gimpy Steph was not playing all that well, and thus, his sneakers looked so much worse.

What a coup for Nike the 2016 Finals was. Not only did LeBron reassert dominance with his incredible series comeback, but victory came with co-Nike pitchman Kyrie Irving nailing one of the biggest shots in NBA history, right in Steph's face. Two images from that Finals stick with me, both involving Lynn Merritt, the Nike power broker and LeBron consigliere. The first was an image of Warriors dominance and Nike frustration. After an easy Warriors victory in Game 2, Merritt remained in the arena, planted at a courtside seat, by himself, just sitting and staring. Lynn was dragooned from his spot by Curtis Jones, the security guard known for passing Steph the ball before he takes a final pregame warmup shot from the sidelines, a famous ritual. Jones, a veteran of the arena courtside space, abides nobody, no matter how powerful, breaking his rules. So Lynn, one of the sport's most powerful and imposing figures, wasn't even allowed his sad meditation. He sheepishly trudged away.

There was no trudging after Game 7, and no court sanctity to be guarded. When an opponent wins a championship on the road, it's as close to a city sacking as we see in civilized society. Your enemy defiles your palace, spraying cheap booze all over the place as they jump around and loudly bellow. Later, they will enter your city's nightclubs in search of women for a victorious romp. There

are no heads on spikes, but there's certainly testosterone-charged merriment, mess, and all-around mayhem in conquered enemy territory. Steph caught some hell when, earlier in the 2015–2016 season, he said the "Cavs visitors' locker room smelled like champagne." That comment cut deep, down to the primal level.

Cleveland's and Nike's revenge came so sweetly in the 2016 Finals. Cavs players walked about the Warriors' court, tracking sticky booze onto the floor. You could hear the Velcro-esque sounds of sneakers decoupling from hardwood. Outside the visitors' locker room, I saw Lynn Merritt again, and my what a different Oracle context. He and LeBron sprayed each other with pink champagne, laughing uproariously, heads tilted to the sky. Old Curtis Jones, stationed by the heartsick Warriors locker area, could not tax Lynn's joy. LeBron was wearing a black Nike shirt that he'd quickly put on upon reaching the locker room. Kyrie was wearing the very same shirt. This wasn't fashion. It was commercialized triumph.

The next blow to Under Armour was already in the works. Unlike what transpired on June 19, 2016, it would be, paradoxically, good for Golden State and terrible for Cleveland. Until this point, what was good for the Warriors was good for Under Armour, as Golden State was their beachhead into the West Coast market.

Kevin Durant, another Nike man, already had designs on leaving the Thunder for the Warriors. KD already had a lot of contact with his supposed enemy squad. The Warriors thought they had an in with Durant, based on Oklahoma City star point guard Russell Westbrook's selfish style of play. The Warriors sold egalitarian fun, in a more enjoyable locale. It was a solid pitch, even if KD would suffer an initial PR hit. Durant was in, far earlier than he'd like many to believe. For months, there was only one man, and one brand, who could potentially hold the plan up, the guy KD

would derisively call "Golden Boy" in his Thunder days, according to Royce Young of the *Daily Thunder* blog. If Steph Curry vocally opposed the move, it could scare Durant off from committing. KD loved to be loved and was looking for a second act that not only elevated but also accepted him. The Warriors needed Steph to buy in to ensure that Durant would buy in.

The Warriors and KD needed Steph to effectively sacrifice industry for team. This wasn't like the Big Three Heat squad, a collaborative dream, forged in friendship. Steph knew KD like he knew a lot of guys in the league, but the two were not close. Golden State had to approach Steph on this potential decision and make the pitch to him. Curry was eventually receptive.

Ever the good soldier, Steph abandoned his Under Armour basketball camp, located in Hawaii, to hop on a plane and fly to the Hamptons. To assure Durant, Steph made sure to say that he didn't care about shoe sales in the meeting. Klay Thompson hilariously cut the tension by asking of Durant's arrival, "Is it good for ANTA?" ANTA, the Chinese shoe brand Thompson endorsed, remains an obscure product stateside, though a fun novelty product to reference.

Nike, who most certainly does care about shoe sales, loved KD's choice. Such machinations don't usually get discussed in the reporting of free agency decisions, but this was too large to ignore. Adrian Wojnarowski tweeted over that summer, after Durant announced his move to the Warriors: "For Nike, this is a coup: It wanted to slow Under Armour's momentum with Steph Curry and Warriors. Now, KD promises to impact Curry's star." In this framing, Kevin Durant, as much as he was a brand unto himself, was serving Nike's purposes in a different way. In business, KD was a kamikaze plane headed straight for The Good Ship Steph. Durant would not be widely lauded for joining a ready-made

seventy-three-win team, and in many spaces he would be criticized. What mattered most to Nike, though, was that Steph Curry was no longer the story.

Durant's first Warriors press conference included much pomp and circumstance. The practice floor had been converted into an amphitheater, packed with more seats than I'd ever seen at Warriors HQ. The left flank of the very front row was all Nike: Lynn Merritt, Chuck Terrell (KD's Nike liaison), Adrian Stelly (Draymond's Nike liaison), and of course, Draymond himself.

Before Durant's introductory Warriors press conference, the last I'd seen KD and Lynn in the same spot was Oklahoma City's Chesapeake Energy Arena, after Durant's Thunder had throttled the Warriors to take a theoretically commanding 3–1 lead in the 2016 Western Conference Finals. Few events are more social than what follows a playoff game, when the crowd is back on the freeway, driving to real life. Player family members, friends, celebrities, and all manner of VIP mill about the empty court, schmoozing as they wait for stars to make the rounds. In this setting, Lynn Merritt is a man about town. He's large, broad-shouldered, with a laugh that booms. It's easy to see how he connects with athletes. That night, Lynn's smile was continuous, as he guided KD from VIP to VIP, with his arm slung around his prized employee's back. This may have been Durant's arena, but this was Lynn's world. And, two months later, it would cease to be Durant's arena.

Merritt was a former liaison, or "sports marketing representative" as they're officially called. Today, Merritt is Nike's VP of Global Basketball Sports Marketing, i.e., King of the Reps. Merritt is atop an odd, charismatic order, a liminal zone that can only exist in the NBA. These reps are usually stylish former players with excellent social skills, who operate almost as hired entourage members to the athletes. They hang out with the players frequently, if

all goes according to plan. The liaisons are points of connection between brand and superstar. As they get close to the superstar, they might even operate as an advocate on behalf of the superstar against certain brand demands. While this might sound like a rather insane arrangement, a company employee who acts as an employee lobbyist within the company, there's a reason this setup exists: the players like it.

What the best players want, the best players get. The same goes for the liaisons to the best. Lynn Merritt was that for a young LeBron James and Merritt accumulated much power at Nike as LeBron's star rose. He was shepherd to a young man, a "father figure" to James as described in a 2008 Brian Windhorst article. Merritt was also something of a protective guardian. During Game 4 of the 2015 Finals, James tumbled into a baseline camera and cut his head. Cameras caught Merritt yelling at the cameraman: "Fucking asshole!" and "It's your fault!"

Merritt had a relationship with Durant, as he did with all of Nike's signature sneaker stars, but KD would never be LeBron to Lynn. In conversations with Nike employees, they'd spoken of Durant's "insecurity" within the company. LeBron was the face of Nike, and KD was something else.

But here Lynn Merritt was, this time in Oakland, beaming as KD held up his new Warriors jersey. I went up to Lynn, who cordially busted my balls for a few minutes, as per usual. I mentioned how I'd seen him celebrating the 2016 Finals win. Lynn bellowed, "And we'll keep celebrating! Got 'em both!"

"Both," meaning both relevant NBA superteams, the Cavs and Warriors. The next Finals would be a Nike affair no matter what. Heads they win, Tails Under Armour loses.

Did Nike influence Durant's choice? KD explicitly denied it. Then again, he was similarly defensive when asked about possibly

leaving the Warriors in 2019. On media day of 2016, when asked if a move to a bigger market helped Nike, Durant said, "Nike, it didn't matter where I played. They didn't care where I played basketball, they support me. We have a great partnership. I didn't let them know until I did it, there wasn't any movement, they just supported me no matter what."

Perhaps he protested too much. Even if you believe the latter part, that the largest corporation in sports was the last to know of their employee's business decision (note: word of Durant's decision was filtering through sources at Nike before the official announcement), it's ridiculous to assert their apathy regarding the outcome. Nike doesn't pay Durant a potential $300 million through 2024 because they like his personality. They pay him to sell shoes. At a minimum, they must have had an opinion about it.

The Warriors and Nike both got their way. The Warriors were better for the choice Steph made and Steph's brand was worse for the making of said decision. Since Curry was no longer the absolute face of the team, and since he was dividing up scoring responsibilities with another superstar, the arrangement did, as Wojnarowski put it, impact Curry's star. Curry maintained his quality of play, but was summarily bumped out of MVP conversations due to his shouldering of a lighter load. Under Armour struggled for a long stretch after the 2016 NBA playoffs debacle. Obviously there are reasons for this beyond Steph, such as the difficulties of going to war with Nike over workout tech. Still, Steph's fame had been something of a bellwether. UA's stock the day before Curry's MCL injury was $46.99. On the opening night of the 2017 NBA season, UA's stock price had since sunk to $16.30. It slowly recovered after that juncture, but the impact of the summer's events was hard to miss. On October 22, 2019, in response to languishing sales and stock value, Under Armour announced that Kevin Plank would

be stepping away from his CEO role in favor of a new position as company brand chief.

Someone in Steph's camp once asked me, "How would you feel about his choice if you were [Under Armour CEO] Kevin Plank?" It was quite literally the first time anyone had asked me to consider the feelings of a billionaire. I suppose not well, especially under the ensuing circumstances.

As Steph was sacrificing individuality for team, he was leveraging his power within Plank's company. Curry's camp won a battle over his shoe's branding, a concession of import to Plank. The side of Steph's shoe had previously brandished the UA logo, derided by sneakerheads as an image that didn't conform to a shoe's profile like the legendary Nike swoosh. Steph lobbied for the Curry 3 to instead carry Curry's personal SC/30 logo. Plank wasn't a CEO that UA had brought in as an outside mercenary. This company was his baby; that logo, his coat of arms. Plank had gone into credit card debt to found UA and had turned his little dream into a billion-dollar concern. But, much like the NBA, the sneaker game calls for billionaires to kowtow to the feelings of twenty-somethings, even on matters of deep symbolism. Steph had the power to make the Under Armour stock fall, all the while still holding enough power over UA to make Plank buckle.

There was friction between the two sides over more than logo placement. In 2017, Curry called an infamous meeting of Under Armour officials to his Alamo, California, home. The ostensible reason was a review of product specs and a marketing plan following a less than successful launch of the Curry 4 shoe and the company's first global layoffs. Officials present did not receive warm and cuddly Steph, he of the persona beloved by fans worldwide. Instead, Steph lit into officials, singling out individuals in the room for coming up short on vision and execution. After perhaps

the fastest rise in NBA history, Steph's off-court status was in stasis as UA scuffled on the basketball front.

In February 2017, Steph delivered a public rebuke of his brand's CEO. Plank was quoted calling Donald Trump "an asset to the country" on CNBC. In response, Steph simultaneously mocked Trump and Plank, telling Marcus Thompson in a Bay Area News Group article, "I agree with that description, if you remove the 'et' from asset." That quote would go viral. Thompson knew what he had the instant Steph said it. Aghast and amused he asked Steph, "Since when did you become such a *gangster*?" Steph was succinct: "Today." Steph would go on to have a famously acrimonious relationship with the forty-fifth president, who threw Twitter tantrums in response.

Plank would go on to tell NBC, "It was unfortunate that my words got characterized in a way that were meant to be divisive in some way, shape, or form." In August, Plank would leave Trump's Manufacturing Council, shortly after Trump's widely criticized comments on the white nationalist march in Charlottesville, Virginia.

Would Steph have spoken so freely if he were still carrying a multibillion-dollar company on his back? Hard to say, but it's easier to be a gangster when you have less to lose. Before he slipped in Houston, before he consented to the recruitment of Durant, Steph had everything, and thus, everything to lose.

Athletes are so competitive that it's easy to assume they'd die for that top spot, and that it means everything to maintain. I'm sure the first part is generally true. I'm less certain about the second part. When I mentioned Steph's sacrifice of status to a top Warriors executive in 2017, he quickly responded, "Did you ever consider, maybe he wanted that?"

At the height of fame, Steph's life had the appearance of an unsustainable whirlwind. Ralph Walker was fond of saying, with

wonderment, "I'm protecting 1985 Michael Jackson right now." So many events, so many screaming fans. Steph, ever the nice guy, sought to meet all the obligations he could. He'd spend so much time after games conversing with a seemingly endlessly flow of friends and acquaintances. "He can't keep doing this," my friend and former ESPN colleague Amin Elhassan exclaimed, upon observing Steph's postgame glad-handing in Phoenix. "I saw Steve Nash at his peak and he couldn't handle a fraction of this. No one has that much energy."

During the two-time MVP years, the surrounding hysteria could get threatening. Steph once tweeted, in August 2015, "PSA. Noticeably following my family's car on the road for nearly 30 miles & tailing me the whole way is not the best way to get an autograph." A couple months later, at a practice at UC San Diego, a couple of autograph seekers leapt out of the bushes in what initially felt like a surprise ambush.

There were upsides to that Number One spot to be sure. His wife, Ayesha, had parlayed the renown into various cooking gigs: a cookbook, TV appearances, and so on. There's certainly an ego boost to being on top of a league that had scoffed at your potential.

But was all of it worth that constant, unrelenting glare of attention that greets singular stars? Was it worth an unyielding weight of expectations? True, KD's presence lessened Steph's luster, but it also mitigated the attached demands. Perhaps it was a bargain for Steph, the human being, though it kneecapped Steph, the brand. In accepting Durant, Curry may have sacrificed sports immortality in exchange for a life. And Under Armour may have lost billions to the cause of work-life balance.

In the end, Kevin Durant's brand was similarly bruised for the joining of forces. It had never quite been this way. Winning championships turns you into a made man, theoretically king of the

zeitgeist. KD couldn't even eclipse Kyrie Irving as a sneaker sales-
man, let alone LeBron.

The 2016–2017 Warriors were impressive, perhaps the greatest
team we've ever seen. Unfortunately for Durant, his team was so
impressive that he came off looking like less of a leader. His lackluster sneaker sales did not help such sentiments.

For the ego, being "the face" of Nike is so much more than
winning a championship. It means you're the biggest athlete on
the planet, a hero known to every country, from the biggest cit-
ies to the tiniest villages. Championships were secured but this
status, the crowning prize of it all, was held just out of reach yet
again. Michael Jordan was the prototype, Kobe was the heir, and
LeBron wasn't leaving. All would have legacy brands, postretirement products that might extend fame and influence to the minds
of humans not yet conceived. Durant was locked out of this club.
He was not the face of Nike. He was a man without a country, an
issue that fueled his want to travel.

In the offseason after Durant won his first Warriors championship, he told Bill Simmons on a podcast, "Nobody wants
to play in Under Armours." Curry responded in his hometown
paper, the *Charlotte Observer*, "Where we were four years ago
and where we are now—you can't tell me nobody wants to wear
our shoes. I know for a fact they do." Curry added, "There is
nothing that is going to put a wrench in our locker room." Those
were simpler times.

5

KEVIN AND ME

I reached out to Kevin Durant for this chapter. The exchange, via text, ended as follows:

> HIM: Fuck u, fuck your sources and your book. How much money you paying me for my chapter?

> ME: Ha, how much you think it's worth?

> HIM: Not enough.

Kevin Durant, the basketball player, is effortless and bound by very little. He believes that there should be more appreciation of his game and he's probably correct. Up until the point at which Durant ruptured his Achilles in Game 5 of the 2019 NBA Finals, much of that appreciation had been undercut and overshadowed by the "noise" Durant either generates, or is the victim of, depending on perspective. The grievous injury allowed fans to simultaneously see his sacrifice for the game and cast doubt on whether we

would ever see him at his best, ever again. As the cliché goes, you don't know what you have until it's gone.

What's gone is, temporarily, a basketball prodigy. KD is a genius on the court, an unprecedented combination of size, skill, and smarts. He is an elite shooter with the handle of a guard and height of a center. That height helps make his shot difficult to block, but there's a quirk to his form that also makes it completely confounding to defend. Though right-handed, Durant's preferred shooting pocket is on the left side of his body. When he receives a pass, he dips the ball on his left side before bringing it back to the right side on the way up. It's not textbook form and that's probably for the best. It's hard to track the ball on its upward loop. Idiosyncratic offense might be countered with idiosyncratic defense. The former comes naturally to KD, and the latter must be learned by his opponents.

It looks like much of basketball comes easily to Kevin Durant, though he does work hard. At peak form, KD can score from odd angles, often off one foot, almost casually in the heat of the moment. The contested midrange jumper has become the bane of NBA offense the past few years, with many a team begging their players to stop taking such low-value shots. For KD, it remained a devastating weapon, a fact that makes him sui generis among scorers. In the 2018–2019 season, Durant would convert 55.1 percent of his midrange attempts. For comparison, his former teammate Russell Westbrook, who also loves jacking from midrange, converted 31.8 percent of such attempts.

In the 2012 NBA Finals, KD dribbled into a midrange fadeaway, and launched over the outstretched arms of Dwyane Wade. After the shot went in, KD removed his mouthpiece and shouted, "Too small!" at the six foot four guard. This was the issue for most defenders agile enough to stay in front of Kevin Durant. They were indeed too small. As for anyone who was tall enough, they also happened to be too slow.

In the unusual circumstance where the defender wasn't too slow or too small, they were often too gullible. KD was savvy with his craft and loved punishing jumpy defenders with baits and feints. He leveraged his odd shooting motion into a foul-drawing weapon so effective that the NBA had to change its rules. Early in his career, Durant pioneered the "rip thru" move, where he'd swing his left-to-right shooting motion under the arms of a too close defensive player. In 2011, the NBA stopped allowing this as an act of shooting foul. Henceforth, it was called as a reach-in foul that wouldn't always be rewarded with free throws. From a December 2011 article by Ben Detrick, writing for *Grantland*: "The most egregious exploiter of the rip-through is easy to single out. Almost by himself, Kevin Durant turned an infrequent incident that lacked any specific name into a problem the league was compelled to address."

The league never quite was prepared for KD. Despite delivering one of the greatest individual seasons in college basketball history as a freshman at Texas, Durant would famously get selected second in the 2007 NBA Draft behind traditional center Greg Oden out of Ohio State. This was not a controversial choice at the time. Greg Oden made sense to GMs in a way KD did not.

Durant was nearly as tall as Oden, and far more skilled, but that made him a man without an obvious position, in an era when basketball was far more constrained by category. Oden was stronger and fit the big man archetype. Plug him in and he solidifies your defense plus interior scoring for a decade, the thinking went. At the time, KD didn't fit anyone's archetype. In this way, he was slighted for being skillful, dismissed because he displayed finesse at a height where brute strength is more commonly demanded.

So Kevin Durant was not an archetypal big man. It turns out he was an unforeseen prototype. KD was a wing unlike any that had come before. Lumbering Greg Oden would go on to be a famous bust of a pick, mostly due to injuries. Kevin Durant would go on

to become one of the greatest scorers the league had ever known. In addition to that, he would be a player without obvious weaknesses. When focused, due to his length, he was as good a defensive player as anyone in the league. His passing and rebounding were both high level. After Dirk Nowitzki's career faded there was no better post scorer in the NBA.

The irony of Kevin Durant joining a superteam is that he perhaps needed the least help of any player to produce individually. He could improve any team in any situation. Unlike other stars, including LeBron James, KD did not even appear to require rhythm or space to score as he desired. When the action bogged down in Warriors playoff games, they would often dump the ball down to KD for a slow, deliberate, unblockable turnaround jump shot. No other team could access such a cheat code at will.

As a young man, Kevin Durant had truly mastered the game. There was no reliable strategy for curbing his impact. He had also chosen the perfect team. Not only was KD unstoppable, but he was flanked with too much talent for teams to even bother trying. Championships would now be earned with the ease that other high-level teams secure playoff berths. Kevin Durant had won it all. And that's when the problems started.

"I remember it like it was yesterday. It was one of the worst moments of my professional career," former Cavs general manager David Griffin said of the day Kevin Durant announced he'd sign with the Warriors in a *Player's Tribune* article titled, "My Next Chapter." "Griff," now GM of the New Orleans Pelicans, had scarcely finished celebrating the best moment of his professional career, the Cavs' historic championship that had occurred two weeks prior.

The Cavs had just laid the Warriors low, coming back from 3–1 to win the title on the Golden State home floor. Steph Curry, perhaps hindered by an injury suffered earlier in the playoffs, was

KEVIN AND ME   89

terrible down the stretch. The game's iconic moment came at his expense when Kyrie Irving hit one of the sport's biggest ever shots over his desperate closeout. With time winding down, the Dubs had erred and panicked. Harrison Barnes sealed defeat with an intentional foul when no foul was called for. The crowd was stunned. The Cavs had made history, conjuring the kind of sports moment you'd hope to live in forever.

There's no playbook for what to do after winning a championship. The commissioner hands you a trophy, you have your parade, you're done. Life should be settled. Conquest over, season over. Let the losers lick their wounds. Let the winners revel in the kind of public drunkenness that winds up on TMZ.

Except, the NBA does not work like this. The overlong schedule demands furious planning in the aftermath of furious on-court action. In 2016, teams had twelve days between the end of the NBA Finals and the hectic July 1 start of free agency.

Also, July 1 is only the start in technicality. You would have to be naive to believe all teams and players are adhering to the league's "tampering" rules. I know general managers who are quite open, at least in private, in stating that contracts are agreed upon before they are "agreed upon." Conversations are always happening, even if they cannot be repeated.

So David Griffin, though still basking in a fairy-tale kind of victory, sauntered into the Cavs war room with an eye toward the future. That's about when the Cavs' future ended. They were braced for what was coming, but it did not lessen the blow.

"I was in our basketball operations room with our whole staff that was gathered for free agency. Our analytics team, our scouts. We're all gathered around the table and our analytics guys are in there. They walk out of the room to run the numbers on what it looks like with KD there. We talked a lot about it, but not necessarily how they'll go about achieving it. Our analytics guy Jon

Nichols walks back in. 'Well, best we can figure the Warriors are supposed to win eighty-three games this year. I think there's some noise in the numbers.'"

That line at least prompted some laughter, a dash of gallows humor to ease the pain. "We were devastated, from an emotional standpoint," Griff said. "We had a period of being extremely disappointed." The Cavs were over, even if they were on the cusp of two more Finals runs. They wouldn't be close to competitive in either of those series.

The Houston Rockets would come closer to felling the KD-era Warriors, losing two series that they seemed to control for a time. Perhaps the Rockets were better prepared for this basketball apocalypse. Their GM, Daryl Morey, had a certain informed fatalism about the whole thing. "I think when I first got a good sense KD was signing in Golden State was in May, at the draft combine in Chicago that year," Morey said. Rockets star James Harden had remained friends with Durant since their days playing together in Oklahoma City. Through certain back channels, Morey had known of Durant's decision months before it became official. Morey thought KD was making the correct, obvious choice. He recalled, "When I heard KD was going there, I said, 'Of course he is.'" Morey couldn't be mad at the Warriors. He and the Rockets had taken a look into whether KD could be recruited to their potential superteam in Houston. "Oh ya," Morey said of chasing Durant. "We're whores."

The KD-to-the-Bay rumblings started in the winter, though many chose not to hear them. The idea of Kevin Durant joining the Warriors, though financially possible, was so inconceivable to so many. It was just too much, too decadent. There was an aversion to believing for all the reasons the move underwhelmed casual fans from its outset. As observers, we often project what we want onto what the players want. But life as a player is radically different

from life as a fan, and the two sides don't understand each other all that well, even in an era of constant public communication. That's how LeBron James could get blindsided by the public's reaction to his "I'm Taking My Talents to South Beach" Decision Special. He and his team were oblivious to how their big gambit might play in the public square. America felt sympathy for the rejected Cavs fans. Players consider themselves the main protagonist in these stories. It's not intuitive to them that the (often fickle) feelings of fans might shape a narrative. James, who "thinks in narrative," according to *LeBron Inc.* author Brian Windhorst, learned from his 2010 gaffe. When he rejoined the Cavs in 2014, much of his rhetoric was rooted in appealing to local sensibilities.

Though James returned and, incredibly, eventually won a championship in Cleveland, there was no guarantee he would be there forever. He had already shown a tendency to leave when a roster gets barren. The Cavs sought to be aggressive with their improvements. They tried to be proactive when they heard the rumors about Durant leaving his team in 2016.

On the one hand, if KD left Oklahoma City and joined the Warriors, it was an apocalyptic event for the Cavs. On the other hand, if KD joined the Cavs, Cleveland could slay the Warriors dragon once and for all. What if KD wanted to join forces with the other best player in the league? "'How could we do it?' we wondered," Griffin said. "Throughout the year, we did some intel, some recon, on how likely is it he would want to play with Kyrie and LeBron. How likely is it he can envision himself living in Cleveland, Ohio?"

It was a nonstarter.

"The answer was 'not very good,'" Griffin said. "The odds were not very good. We had another sit-down and come-to-Jesus in February around the trade deadline because that's when we would have needed to act on things. That's when we'd have to upset the apple cart."

Had Durant opted for joining his fellow Nike stars in Cleveland, All-Star power forward Kevin Love would have needed to be traded. In this way, Durant had the power in winter of 2016 to derail what ultimately became the first Cavs championship season. Had he signaled an early interest in Cleveland, Griffin would have been compelled to blow up a title-level roster in anticipation for his arrival the next season. It just so happened that whatever Kevin Durant was seeking was not in Cleveland, Ohio.

Lee Jenkins, then at *Sports Illustrated*, would refer to Durant as "a searcher" in an interview on Colin Cowherd's sports talk show. That search appeared perpetual for the fundamentally inscrutable superstar.

There's another term for what Kevin Durant is, in the NBA parlance: he's a "Different Dude." The NBA has its share of Different Dudes. It's long been a home for the iconoclastic personality disproportionately found among those who can channel a certain improvised freedom at the height of competition. It's a sport that celebrates and markets such special individual creators, elevating them above their teams. All the while, that team still operates according to the tenets of quasi militaristic jock culture, wherein others must fit in and keep their heads down. So there's a natural tension between team concept and the team's reality of being beholden to the whims of a certain individual. That individual, clothed in immense power at the age of twenty something, might become more brand than man, thrust into a circumstance apart from and beyond the teammates he depends on. Such a rarefied alienation is a recipe for Different Dudeness. The NBA superstar is often a mystifying man whose powers just happen to be worth the quirks. Honestly, in the modern social media–driven NBA, you're lucky if the soft-spoken rookie you drafted doesn't turn into Howard Hughes with a handle. "They're all fucking crazy now," one NBA coach said to me, when

lamenting how his profession had changed. "All the superstars are fucking crazy."

I first met Kevin Durant in a hookah bar on Geary Street in San Francisco, the night before a preseason home game. It was somewhat by happenstance. I was there with a friend, looking into a story that had nothing to do with Durant. Ultimately I didn't find what I was looking for, but I did run into San Francisco's most hyped new resident. He walked in with his agent Rich Kleiman and strolled into 724's humble, cozy VIP area.

Many NBA stars are hookah heads, surprising as this may sound. They are up later than you and occasionally require a more relaxing social activity. In the end, all that theoretically lung-pickling hookah smoke is hardly an obstacle to greatness. Legend has it that this spot's cachet spread by word of mouth from Shaq to Kevin Garnett and then to everyone else.

So here we were, now in early October, with the season about to start. The VIP area is fairly open at 724, a nice mix between cordoned-off and visible. I introduced myself and shook hands over the velvet rope. "You know how we feel about you mother-fuckers at ESPN!" KD teased. Then he paused. "Ah, get in here," he said, motioning me into the lounge. Rich and KD were nice enough to invite my buddy in as well.

We would hardly be the last invited into the room. It was Fleet Week in San Francisco, and the lounge was replete with naval officers. KD started inviting them into the VIP area and didn't stop. If this was my first impression of the man, it was one of a considerate, gregarious extrovert. Look at him go, man about town in his newly adopted home! He was making everyone's night and seemed to be loving that.

Not quite. Kevin was friendly, but more quietly curious than effervescent. The officers and I shared a hookah, but Kevin had one to himself that he was demolishing as he sank into the cushy seats.

He wanted to know these officers. He asked about their lives and contrasted their experiences with his own. There was one young man who, at age twenty-three, was running a warship. Kleiman, languidly puffing on an e-cigarette while reclined like the *Alice in Wonderland* caterpillar, kept telling the kid how impressive he was. I too was wowed. Though this guy was small in stature in addition to the youth, I doubt he ever got carded. There was no gravel in his voice, or aloof masculine posturing. He was actually quite friendly, clean-shaven, and framed with a moderately dorky crew cut. But you could tell. This guy had purpose, a self-possession. He was comfortable in his own skin, stolid in a way that seemed of another era. Maybe he had too heavy a burden to weigh himself down further with millennial ennui.

KD wanted to document knowing this guy, and had him pose for a photo he sent to his close friend DeAndre Jordan, whom the officer readily admitted to having never heard of. KD playfully flipped DJ the bird and asked the officer to join in, which he obliged, a bit awkwardly. The officer started asking Kevin about himself. "What's it like to play in the NBA?"

"It's cool. I worked really, really hard for this," KD said. Then he made a wistful pivot. "You know, soon I'll be thirty, and guys like Ethan will start saying I'm old, and then it will end." He trailed off. Nobody quite knew how to take that one. I'd been around star athletes, but there was a weightiness to KD that I'd not yet encountered. I'd known openly melancholic people, but seldom were they the center of attention like this. I dismissed the oddness as possibly a function of recent media coverage. He wasn't happy about it. Neither was Rich. The press was largely unimpressed with his choosing to join an already stacked, seventy-three-win team. At Durant's first preseason game in Vancouver, he was booed lustily.

The outside world had problems with KD. Meanwhile, these officers were just delighted by his presence. Those who like Kevin

Durant are quite drawn to the side of him I saw in that hookah bar. There are Thunder officials who feel betrayed by his choice, led on and lied to, but who still say, at the end of it all, "I can't help it. I love that kid."

Even some of the Warriors people he's exhausted with his brooding begin their KD-based gripes with, "You know, he's not a *bad* guy." There's just such a magnetic quality to his happiness when it's present. He's got a brimming smile and disarming curiosity. Beyond that, he's got *takes*, opinions on all matters in and around the NBA. It's ironic that he so disdains sports-talk media culture because, if he so chose, he would fit right in and do quite well. I can say, when I did ask him questions, I valued his ability to analyze the league in a way people like me cannot. He was generous with his insight too, and he seemed to enjoy offering it.

In between, the basketball was great. The 2016–2017 Warriors may have been the best team of all time, or at least the most talented. Durant's arrival was fresh, and the peripheral role players had yet to age out. The stars were either in the front or mid-part of their primes. "You know," Bob Myers said, in the preseason of 2018. "That was the first season going in where I *knew* we were winning the championship."

It wasn't so easy, in part because Durant suffered an MCL injury against the Wizards in DC on March 1, 2017, when Zaza Pachulia tumbled into his leg. In pregame that evening, there was an absurd bad omen that foreshadowed future division. KD searched around the locker room in a frenzy, unable to find his Bubba Gump shrimp pouch. "Did you eat my shrimp pouch!" he yelled at Draymond. "Man, what do you think I am, twelve years old!" Draymond responded. "I ain't eat your shrimp pouch!"

Despite being undershrimped and suffering a significant injury, KD came back in the playoffs at the peak of his game. The Warriors would suffer only one loss that entire postseason run,

a forgettable performance after having gone up 3–0 against what was, perhaps, the best Cavs team of the LeBron era. KD gleefully celebrated his first championship, spreading the love on video, giving compliments to end-of-bench teammates and staffers. If he hadn't achieved sustainable happiness, he certainly had locked it in for a moment. Then a summer passed. Still, there was no grand reordering of the consensus: LeBron was still widely considered the league's best player, at Nike and on the floor.

In an ESPN article titled "What Does Kevin Durant Want?" Zach Lowe recounted how Durant was not fulfilled by his first championship. "He didn't have a great summer," former two-time MVP and current Warriors consultant Steve Nash told Lowe. "He was searching for what it all meant. He thought a championship would change everything, and found out it doesn't. He was not fulfilled. He didn't work out as much as he normally does."

The next season wasn't so smooth. The Warriors gave sub-optimal effort on many nights, as could be expected for a squad that knew playoffs to be the true measure of success. The ensuing postseason provided a scare, after Andre Iguodala went down with a "spider fracture" in the Western Conference Finals against the Rockets. Durant was drifting, disengaged on defense as the Warriors tumbled to a 3–2 deficit. The Warriors would fall down big in the next two elimination game victories, eventually snatching victory from the jaws of defeat each time. Durant would wake up in the second half of Game 7 and nail impossible-to-defend shots to end it all. "It looked like we were coming unglued," Kerr said after the game, shaking his head in shock.

The Warriors would win another championship, in Cleveland, but this time the celebration was softer. New title winner Nick "Swaggy P" Young put his teammate's restraint into stark relief. Young started yelling that he would now go by "Swag Champ!" as he stomped around the booze-flooded visitors' locker room carpet.

There weren't as many Warriors in the locker room as there were the first time around. They'd quickly filtered out to other parts of the arena, doing the necessary interviews. Steph walked down the hallway, yelling of another championship, "Every one of them great!" Maybe he believed it, maybe he didn't. It was just hard to buy that this celebration carried the emotional payload of past titles.

The 2018 championship parade brought out the first hints of awkwardness that would in many ways define the next season. It would be the last season to feature the Hamptons Five. Warriors play-by-play man Bob Fitzgerald was MCing the championship festivities and, though not exactly adroit comedically, decided to go in for some jokes. "I heard you tell Kevin Durant he could have whatever contract he wants next year," Fitzgerald told Bob Myers. "That was just for the media," Myers ribbed. "He can't have anything like that at all," Myers added. Kerr interjected, saying "Midlevel," a reference to a modest kind of NBA contract allowance.

"I think last year you told Steph [Curry] he could have any contract he wants, too," Fitzgerald said, not letting it go while referencing Curry's "supermax" $200 million contract.

"Yeah, that was different," Myers replied. "He's been here from the way-before days. He's earned it." The players looked palpably uncomfortable.

"And there ended the Warriors' cohesion, right there," Fitzgerald said.

Internally, some higher-level staffers were angry at Fitzgerald. Truth be told, though, Myers was equally culpable in flicking that bruise. It didn't set the tone for the 2018–2019 season all on its own, but it revealed some of the tension that was starting to set in, even as the confetti was still falling.

The offseason passed without any serious problems. In fact, the team acquired all-NBA forward DeMarcus Cousins, putting

another scare into the rest of the league. He was coming off an injury and wouldn't play for months, but his addition felt like conspicuous consumption all the same.

But soon after the basketball resumed in earnest, the internal strife was on display again. On November 12, 2018, in Los Angeles, Durant cut into Green after Draymond failed to pass him the ball on a bungled end-of-regulation play. He challenged Draymond's pride, which prompted Green to go nuclear. Draymond would call KD a "bitch" multiple times and assail him for dangling his impending free agency over everyone else. In the aftermath, attempts at reconciliation were made. The two continued to work together. But the incident served as a kind of demarcation point. Perhaps the Warriors season was already there, just not so publicly. The event, though, darkened it. It was an incident Kerr expressed concerns about at the time, using the following metaphor when asked about the incident: "Sometimes, team chemistry is like a balloon. You worry about if there's a point where it pops." The argument made news, locally and nationally. In the story of a dynasty, there are only two modes: rise and fall.

The game after KD and Draymond's famous November feud, I asked Andre Iguodala about it. "Shaq and Kobe ain't like each other," he said matter-of-factly. I responded, "But that ended in a way you wouldn't want this to end, right?" Andre replied, "They won three championships in a row. Ain't that what you want to happen?" "I guess all things come to an end," I said. Andre nodded and put a bow on the brief conversation: "Everything come to an end."

What followed was a dragging kind of regular season, one in which the Warriors managed to get a one seed, absent much apparent esprit de corps. Such was their advantage over the league that this qualified as underperforming. More than the basketball, it was just the overall vibe that brought down onlookers. Just as

KD's better moods can be contagious, his worse ones can be the bad kind of infectious. This was a regular season in which Kevin Durant was halfway out the door and in no way loving that status.

In January 2019, I wrote about how the Warriors worked hard to make Kevin Durant happy, in terms of offensive approach. A mutual friend told me that Kevin was livid over the article, so I braced for conflict. Some stars can get mad over a headline. I'd been on the receiving end of that. A couple sentences into the dressing down and you realize it's all based on a tweet. You ask if they read the article and receive a, "I don't HAVE to read the fucking article to . . . " And so forth.

Not KD. He reads everything and takes issue with specific sentences and phrases. A few in particular had inspired his ire, or so I heard. So I entered the Golden 1 Center in Sacramento with certain expectations.

I figured I might get a muttered, "Hater in the house," a phrase KD favors with the disfavored. In any event, I was primed for an interesting exchange. We, the huddled media, received our permission to enter the arena court and trudged on in. It's common at a shootaround to walk onto the floor, in the out-of-bounds area. The moment my feet touched hardwood, a practicing Kevin Durant ditched his shooting drill, and speed-walked in my direction.

The ball KD abandoned was still bouncing when he spat, "How can you write that shit!?" He was off and running, venting about the article as media members gawked on. I went into the autopilot mode I've developed over the years. You can never argue your way out of these, or at least I never had any luck with it. The star will never say, "Gee, that's a good point you made," or, "Ohhhh, I now see that's a metaphor." So I tend to drone, "What's your perspective?" and wait it out, in case some of that perspective comes through and I learn something. Maybe they'll express a truth I

need to grasp. Maybe they'll experience catharsis. I just know this tends to be a one-way street. KD inveighed that I didn't know what I was talking about, and that I didn't know him. Finally, he closed as his voice rose, with a slight tremble. "You don't know me! You don't know what makes me *happy!*"

The media peanut gallery heard that last line. It was too loud and too strange to forget. Among colleagues, the catchphrase would follow me the rest of the season. Anytime I offered an idea on where to get something to eat before the game I was liable to get, "You don't know what makes me happy!" in response.

Later that same day, I showed up to pregame locker room availability. The Old Media Code dictates that, if you've pissed someone off, you have to be available. I suppose it's about accountability and honor, such as we have any in this business. So there I was, available, staring at the TV of an empty locker room. ESPN's Nick Friedell, just before leaving the locker room, mentioned that KD was glaring at me from the training table behind the locker room. Great.

KD made his way from the training table to his locker. He motioned me over with a hurried gesture. Maybe, in retrospect, this interaction could have gone better. I sometimes wonder if what is sought in these matters is mere apologetics. That if I only cave and grovel, we actually get somewhere approximating peace. That certainly isn't the Old Media Code, but it is likely the most expedient process.

I started with that. "Look, I appreciate you being direct with me . . . " But the olive branch was instantly swatted aside, interrupted by more venting. He was big on how I had not included comments from his postgame press conference. He kept repeating this. It confused me, because he was talking fast without context. He assumed I knew everything he'd said in that press conference, including whatever detail he believed pertinent to the article.

His perspective on the matter wasn't wholly insane. If my job is to follow him around and tell stories about what he says, then I must have archival knowledge of everything he says publicly. It doesn't quite work that way, though, at least not for me. Typically, I'll attend the coach press conference, before the locker room is open. The player press conferences that follow happen concurrent with locker room availability. I generally prefer the locker room to the pressers because there's actually a chance I might get information nobody else has. Also, there's just a better shot at seeing something hilarious or having a memorable conversation. Press conferences are usually a bore.

I started responding. "Look, I think . . . " But KD interrupted me, and just in the way I'm used to. He swiveled his head around the locker room. "Not so *loud*, bro," he said. "Everybody don't need to be hearing this." Confused, I whipped my head around, seeing nary a threat. Quinn Cook, an affable friend of Kevin's, was next to us, but the Kings' impressively capacious locker room was otherwise empty. Why was KD worried about our conversation getting overheard by teammates when he wasn't even establishing that this was off record? What was the big problem here?

I tried to make a few points, saying I didn't begrudge him for having leverage with his contract, and insisted that I had good reason to write what I wrote. KD wasn't impressed and accused me of trying to "rile up Steph's fans." He expressed that this was a constant theme in the Bay. All of us local guys just wanted to kiss Steph's ass at his expense. This was KD's consistent lament. He would frequently squabble in direct-message conversations with the Warriors fans of Twitter, frequently accusing them of favoring Steph at his expense. In one such exchange that foreshadowed things to come, he was asked by the WarriorsWorld account whether two-time MVP Steph Curry or Kyrie Irving was the better player. "I gotta really sit down and analyze it," Durant demurred.

I ended up telling KD that, if this kind of thing made him mad, I could actually come to him next time and get his perspective on it before running with something. A reasonable request maybe, but for the athlete, it just promises more interactions with the person they currently despise. KD curtly told me, "Just do your fucking job," and walked off. I looked and shrugged at Cook, who laughed uncomfortably.

Well, it was time to do my job, whatever that is. What it sometimes is, is bullshitting around a basketball court as players warm up. Pregame offers the opportunity to walk about the court and schmooze about the NBA cafeteria scene. I shook hands with Warriors broadcaster Jim Barnett and talked about the advance scouting profession for a spell. I joked around with Warriors assistant coaches. Afterward, Friedell told me that KD was glaring at me through his whole warmup routine. I didn't know what made him happy, but I was getting a sense of what could make him obsessively pissed.

Guys had gotten mad at me before, but not like this. They'd shown anger, but betrayed no obsession. Generally, you get a blast of scorn, but the underlying idea is that you're a pissant who, after the initial transgression, isn't worth a further thought. KD made you feel as though he thought more about you than the other way around. He almost flattered you with his spite. Or, it would be flattering if the spite wasn't so KD-focused. You were only hated insofar as how you reflected on him.

On February 5, 2019, I wrote an article in reaction to KD's eight-day disappearance from media obligations. It wasn't a disappearance that personally offended me; it just seemed meaningful in the grand scheme of that season. I'm sure taking five minutes of media questions is rather boring, but it isn't especially challenging—at least, not in the Bay Area. The Warriors had won a lot and the weather is perfect. We mostly ask these guys what it's

like to win so goddamned much. Fun? Super fun? Good, great, let's go home.

In the middle of the absence, the New York Knicks opened up cap space by trading away their young star Kristaps Porzingis. At that point, many league insiders would talk of KD going to New York as a fait accompli. By Day 6, national media was starting to notice Kevin's disappearance and connect certain dots. This subject had already been looming over the season. So, after reaching out to KD's representation (no response), I wrote up a piece.

The article, titled "Silent Star: On the Presumed Exit of Kevin Durant," broached that subject and some others. It contained the following summarizing paragraph:

> Most people within the Warriors either think Durant is leaving or profess not to know one way or the other. His teammates recognize this reality, can handle it and merely want one outcome: Win a championship, absent too much drama. The main concern, at the moment, is whether he'll commit in the short term to what he may have already left in the long term.

That paragraph was somewhat provocative, in the sense of making public what so many were discussing in private. At the same time, I'm not certain if it's what actually set Kevin Durant off. If I had to guess, I would go with the following passage:

> Sources say that Durant believed his besting of LeBron James in the 2017 Finals would get him hailed as the game's top player, a mantle he's craved for some time. While LeBron averaged a 33.6 point-per-game triple-double in that Finals, Durant was superior defensively and hit the series' biggest shot right in the King's face. Instead, there was no grand reordering of rankings, and only so much credit to be had for a dominant playoff run. KD,

who was "tired of being second" way back in 2013, was still stuck there reputationally, even in ultimate victory. He was still behind LeBron in the eyes of pundits, basketball Twitter, and perhaps most importantly, at Nike, who's employed Durant longer than any team. Then, the next Finals unfolded in much the same way, with much the same result, all while Warriors fans cheered loudest for the smaller MVP's baskets.

There was only so much use in discussing that Kevin Durant might leave without discussing the "why." The "why" was, in part, a reason that couldn't be admitted to, even if he complained to teammates about this particular reason.

The etiquette of sport just wouldn't allow it. We want players to be highly competitive but not to betray any insecurity over their place in a pecking order. So, superstars never say things like, "I'm going to a new team to burnish my reputation and satiate my ego," even if that's the plan exactly.

I was also sympathetic to Durant's reputational plight, insofar as I can feel badly for the moderately held up ambitions of the rich and famous. When I talked to Cavs staffers about the 2017 Finals, they were upfront about how KD had outplayed LeBron. One went so far as to tell me, "Kevin Durant kicked LeBron's ass. He completely dominated LeBron in the series. Every time KD needed to score, he did and it didn't matter what the fuck LeBron did. I was amazed coming out of that series that there wasn't far more discussion of, 'Has KD supplanted LeBron as best player in the world?'"

That public conversation never really happened. It didn't happen the next season either, after Durant had earned another Finals MVP. It mostly didn't happen because nobody wanted it to. By choosing the Warriors, Durant had become a man without a country. Fans in Oklahoma City resented him for what they regarded

as a betrayal. Fans in the Bay Area preferred the little guy and always would. Sure, they'd defend KD against the slights of outsiders, but ultimately he wasn't their favorite. They also didn't trust him. You can't keep signing one-year deals and expect unyielding fealty from a fan base.

This outcome was logical but may have been confusing for KD. When LeBron pissed off the entire country by choosing, famously, "to take [his] talents to South Beach," success had ultimately redeemed him. When LeBron's superteam won a championship against Kevin Durant's 2012 Thunder squad, James was served up a coronation. He was regarded as the best, even by his haters. "Stacking the deck" with fellow stars did not prevent LeBron from claiming his rightful throne. Why did it go differently for KD?

Fans know the answer to that question, even if it's not readily apparent to certain players. The Warriors weren't the 2010 Cavs. They'd just won seventy-three games. It was obvious to observers that the Miami Heat needed LeBron's best efforts to win a championship. With KD? Not as apparent. The Warriors still boasted a world-beating record in the games Durant missed. Many pondered whether the Warriors would be fine if KD's slot were manned by a merely competent small forward, instead of one of the very best ones ever. We want our heroes tested. The Warriors experience seemed more like a testing of player boredom.

Kevin Durant *was* being tested, in certain ways. He had to sacrifice at times, to defer. If he choked, the world would have come down on him in the way LeBron had experienced after the 2011 NBA Finals. When he came through, on the biggest stage, it was taken for granted. Of course he succeeded. He was set up to succeed. In this way, Kevin Durant might have been winning in a no-win situation.

My secret empathy did not count for much. If there was anything I knew about KD by that point, it was that the greatest libel

often was the truth. Not only was Kevin Durant insecure, but he was especially insecure about his insecurities.

By that point, in February 2019, I knew enough about Kevin to know what might come next. I appeared in the locker room pregame, figuring there was a chance the storm would hit early. He walked past, not glancing back at me, as other media people looked on. "Maybe he'll just choose to ignore it?" I thought, idly. Deep down, I knew that wasn't true. KD likes to express himself, usually to the world.

After the game, we media schlubs trundled into the locker room. After gathering his things, KD suddenly bounced upward and made a decisive quick-walk toward the press conference room. I followed twenty paces behind.

I actually don't remember much of the press conference, other than it was fairly tense in the room. When asked about the noise around free agency, KD said:

It's unnecessary. You have a dude, Ethan Strauss, who come in here and just give his whole opinion on stuff and make it seem like it's coming from me. He's just walking around here, don't talk to nobody, just walk in here and survey, then write something like that. Now y'all piling on me because I don't want to talk about that. I have nothing to do with the Knicks, I don't know who traded [Kristaps] Porzingis. They've got nothing to do with me. I'm trying to play basketball. Y'all come in here every day, ask me about free agency, ask my teammates, my coaches, rile up the fans about it. Let us play basketball, that's all I'm saying. And now when I don't want to talk to y'all, that's a problem on me. C'mon man, grow up. Grow up. Yeah, you grow up. I come in and go to work every day. I don't cause no problems. I play the right way, or I try to play the right way. I try to be the best player I can be every possession. What's the problem? What am I doing to y'all?

The journos in the room understood that the moment would go viral, as we are now used to the rules of the press conference panopticon. Anything confrontational will become news fodder. I immediately took certain precautions. In the recent past, reporters at the center of controversies had drawn vicious fan comments on social media posts of family photos, including insults directed at the appearance of wives and children. I wasn't too keen on that happening to my family, so I checked into our security on that end. My phone started buzzing with alerts, as people kept attempting to friend me on LinkedIn. I braced myself for something, but wasn't sure what that something was.

In the meantime, I wrote a response to KD's comments. The main thrust of the response was that the press conference rant just seemed like an extravagant distraction. We were now going to have some big conversation about how put-upon NBA stars are by media coverage (perhaps!), instead of focusing on the actual subject: that the top free agent looks like he wants to leave the top team.

I wrote:

By the way, you'd think team play would be the natural focus of everyone right now. The Warriors might boast the greatest starting lineup the sport has ever seen. They are rolling, having won 13 of their last 14. And yet, in a 39-point victory, Kevin Durant has amplified the story he theoretically wants smothered. He's shining a laser pointer at a July calendar page and bemoaning that anyone dares see the bouncing beam. This is what he does, for reasons that mystify beyond the simple fact that he can. A man with all the leverage can keep speaking in contradictions and reliably keep hearing in supplications.

I ended the article by plugging the book you're currently reading. If that plug in any way informed your decision to buy this

book, get back to me, let me know. The chaos from that week will all have been worth it.

Of course, my opportunistic response did nothing to quiet the controversy. Soon after Durant's rant, Steph Curry offered support for his teammate. "Honestly, I think it's him not being able to control his own voice," Curry said. "He's focused on basketball, and that's what he should do. We want to see that KD every day. What he can't control is BS that happens in the media or people making the decision for him or all this other stuff."

I, too, was about to see what it's like to have your words and intentions debated, absent much control from the subject. I was about to get a taste of my own medicine. I was about to enter The Take Zone.

KD's press conference was the top sports story that following day, replayed over and over on ESPN. It's a dizzying thing to be sports talk fodder, to be dunked into the fishbowl you write about from a slight remove. You wake up, and then slowly remember that you're in the news. There's a creeping sense that you're in charge of some reputation management project, but there's no manual on what to do. Maybe you ignore the project, and delete your social media apps so as to avoid the topic altogether. That doesn't really work because your friends, some of whom you haven't spoken to in years, start texting you snippets of what people on TV are saying. Dan Patrick praised you, and so you watch the clip of Dan Patrick praising you. You feel momentarily warm, fulfilled, validated. You ruminate on how enjoyable 1990s *SportsCenter* was and how Dan has made such a dignified second act as a respectable talk radio star. What a guy, Dan Patrick.

Another friend says that Tracy McGrady criticized you and that it was very unfair. You watch the clip and feel a pang of something sour. There's nothing you can do about this. Also, you feel a strong need to note that Tracy never made it out of the first round

of the playoffs as a relevant player. "Tracy McGrady, what an ass-hole," you tell yourself.

It doesn't end there. There are more pundits, a constant supply of strangers who either balm or needle your insecurities. You rise and fall with the commentary you can't control. The texts keep coming, so there's no escape from You, even if you wanted one. If you wish to use your phone, say, to continue important communication with your wife about the day's schedule, you're in for an inundation of You. There's no avoidance possible, if you wish to live in modernity. Waste is spilling into the ego's reservoir no matter what. Only the Luddite, with his off-the-grid rainwater buckets, can sufficiently guard peace of mind.

Following your reputation is a path to madness. Deep down I'd always known there was a dark side to the narcissism that keeps me checking Twitter mentions, but my defects were never so obvious as when scaled up like this. Your heart pounds as you watch these clips of talking heads debating your reputation. There's a unique frustration to seeing a discussion about you take place, absent your own participation. In the end, there's no satisfying conclusion or catharsis. It just keeps going. I went through this for half a day before detaching, insofar as I could. I'm lucky enough to have a solid base in my life and raison d'être beyond my work. Time with my wife and baby provided perspective. And perhaps most importantly, it ended after a few days. Slowly but surely, the noise quieted, and I escaped The Take Zone.

Kevin Durant lives in The Take Zone. This isn't a secret. KD was, embarrassingly, caught defending his own honor via burner accounts on social media. He frequently lashed out at critics on Instagram. I know fans who received his wrath in their Twitter direct messages. In the locker room, when I was "just walking around here," he'd often be bitching about something a random Twitter user said.

If you squint, it's almost endearing. To lower oneself in raging at the people is adjacent to being a man of the people. KD gave his haters far more consideration than Derek Jeter did his many admirers.

In another era, we might have even seized upon examples of KD's insecurity as an explanation for greatness. Maybe this drove him in the way Michael Jordan was fueled by small slights. According to legend, Jordan once cheated at cards to beat an old woman. This is unhealthy behavior, laughed off as quirky, if not laudable in the context of the singularly accomplished man. We don't draw a line between genius and madness, so much as we insist that the former is winsome.

Truly, no slight was too small for Durant. In the Phoenix road game following the "Grow Up" incident, KD confronted *San Francisco Chronicle* beat writer Connor Letourneau. Connor's crime? Over forty minutes into a podcast, he'd offered a theory on why KD might want to follow Kyrie Irving to the Knicks. You might wonder, was this podcast hosted by Stephen A. Smith, or some other titan of the industry? Not exactly. *Warriors Huddle* is hosted by two genial basketball fans for whom this is a hobby.

Of the standoff, visible to other media members present, Letourneau said, "I'm just standing in the locker room near the door, on my phone and he is walking out of the locker room and he stops and he looks at me and he just goes, 'Have I been good to you?'"

Letourneau was confused, knowing nothing of what this was about. "I'm like, 'What do you mean have you been good to me?' And he just keeps repeating himself over and over, 'Have I been good to you? Have I been good to you?' He's kind of creeping towards me, and I have no idea what he's upset about at this point. I have no idea what's going on. Over the course of a few minutes, I end up having a back-and-forth with him. I ask, 'What's going

on? What's your issue?' And he basically tells me, 'You're over here talking shit behind my back.'"

This was a feature of bad KD interactions. If he was mad at you, he expected you to know the exact context as to why, even if it wouldn't make intuitive sense.

"I ask, 'What are you talking about?' He goes, 'You're over here questioning my motives, acting like you know me. You don't know me like that.'"

Once Letourneau got to the heart of the conflict, he was shocked.

"I end up talking to him in the hallway. It becomes clear to me that he's referencing a podcast that I went on, *The Warriors Huddle* podcast, which is a local podcast. It has a following in the Bay Area, but not a national podcast by any means. I'd gone on with a couple friends of mine and they were asking if Durant leaves for New York, what will be his reasoning? I basically said, he will go with Kyrie to try and team up with Kyrie and follow Kyrie."

Letourneau laughed as he recalled the absurdity. But that was life with Kevin Durant.

In my experience, when players are angry about something you've written or said, they don't want to give you the satisfaction of knowing that they were checking up on you. "Someone sent it to me" is a common explanation. Not so with Kevin, as Durant would make clear to Letourneau in a closing admonition.

"KD said, 'I hear and I read *everything*. And don't forget that.' He said it multiple times."

The local media was a constant source of frustration for Durant. He wanted to be feted and was highly sensitive to the praise or lack of criticism that teammates received. On the March road trip, Klay had a big game and opted out of doing media that evening. Letourneau recalled, "Ray Ridder went in there and asked, 'Where's Klay?' Klay dipped out through the back door

and avoided his media obligations. Durant looked at all of us and asked, 'You guys gonna write about that? You're not, are you, because anything Klay does is okay because it's Klay. But anything I do is not okay because I'm Kevin Durant.' That was not the only time he complained about how Klay was treated, because he felt that Klay got a free pass for everything."

It wasn't just positive coverage of Klay that bothered KD. Letourneau said, "He got annoyed in Dallas when we were asking about Luka Doncic. At the time Luka had more points than him in the All-Star voting and that really pissed him off. It was clear in his comments about Luka that he didn't feel Luka was deserving of that. At the same time it's like, dude, who cares?"

You did not have to be a star or rising star to draw KD's envious ire. When former Warriors bench scorer Marreese Speights returned to Oracle Arena, he got a hearty ovation from the crowd. "Mo Buckets" had been a fan favorite, in part due to his tremendous shooting streaks and also due to the broad smile he beamed when riding such a wave. He wasn't a flawless player but his enthusiasm was infectious and the fans were nostalgic for it. KD— who once complained to a Warriors fan account over Twitter DM that Speights was among the players more accepted by Warriors fans than he—was not pleased.

After the blowout Warriors win that followed, as he waited to take the podium stage, Durant was fixated on a TV that hung from the wall. Speights was with the local TV guys, yukking it up. "Mo Buckets," Durant loudly groused, shaking his head. "How can you call yourself 'Mo Buckets' when you never averaged twenty points a game?"

Durant had a habit of slighting even the most random of other players' accomplishments. When he aired his objections it often drew laughter from media, under the presumption that this was all a joke, a light razzing of a friend.

Sometimes it was, but even those moments could reveal certain sensitivities. On Sirius NBA Radio, ESPN's Amin Elhassan and *The Athletic*'s Zach Harper riffed off this premise to much amusement. After DeMarcus Cousins made his long-awaited return from an Achilles tear, he exceeded expectations by scoring 14 points in his return game and thus was awarded the game ball. From Marcus Thompson's game story that night:

"How you score 14 points and you keeping the game ball?" Durant said, needling his teammate in the visiting locker room. "You ain't score 50. What's it gon' say—14 points in 15 minutes?

"Hell yeah," Cousins said loudly as he slapped fives with Durant. "I'm writing it on there. I'm painting it and every thang."

Elhassan and Harper had fun with Durant's contention, joking about whether KD was indeed serious about the game ball. The segment was funny enough that Sirius NBA cut a promotional ad from the exchange and posted it on social media. Sources within Sirius claim that hours later, the Warriors voiced their displeasure and conveyed that Sirius NBA would be getting no Warriors guests at All-Star Weekend. The promotion was pulled. Historically, the Warriors have a very accommodating PR department. It's highly unlikely such a move happened without a lot of pressure coming from one player in particular. Harper and Elhassan were joking, and maybe Durant had been too. Still, the duo had cut too close to the bone.

The home game after "Grow Up" was another experience. As goes the Old Media Code, I had to be available, yet again. I sauntered in for pregame media availability. I saw Kevin at his corner locker, on his phone as per usual. Every player looked at their phone a fair amount, but with KD, it was as though the device was an extension of his fingernails. After games, the time when guys

typically tease one another and revel in the events of the past four quarters, Durant was often seated, by himself, staring and scrolling. This time, he was locked into his device in pregame.

When KD finally put the phone down and got up, I approached. "You wanna talk?"

"How the fuck can you come up and talk to me!" he responded while moving briskly.

"You're the one saying I don't talk to you," I replied.

"The only time you can talk to me is in a scrum!" Kevin shot back.

I was a little amused, having never heard a player use the word "scrum." Players are always getting shuttled to scrums, but you don't ever hear them talk about scrums. Anyway, I'd done my job. I'd been available, faced the music, abided by the Old Media Code. It was nearly time to leave the locker room and resume life as persona non grata.

"Ethan! Get over here!" My ears perked up, but I couldn't see where the voice was coming from. I scanned the room and saw Andre Iguodala, half hidden behind a locker room hallway. "Get over here, Ethan!"

Andre then decisively pulled me into the Player's Lounge. I always liked Andre but didn't know what to expect. This wasn't covered in the Old Media Code manual.

In this job, you become very accustomed to the rules regarding space. You're always allowed in the media room, and allowed a few other places within specific time frames. Your media pass grants access to anywhere in the stands. The interview room would be open at all times except for when it's converted into a chapel that players attend pregame. Even the sanctified locker room is open to media, most often between 6:15 and 6:45 p.m. But the Player's Lounge in the back of the locker room? Never.

I looked up and saw big man Kevon Looney, who was already giggling. Andre had a way of cracking up young Kevon. Beside

him was Jonnie West, youngest son of Jerry West and classic Basketball Ops man. Jonnie fit in around the players because he'd grown up in this world. Additionally, Jonnie was also a scratch golfer, and therefore a frequent greens companion to Andre and Steph Curry. In that moment, I envied his ease of place.

Andre stood before me and asked, "Did you apologize?"

I wanted to be sure of what we were talking about. "Apologize for what?" I said.

With exasperation, Andre repeated, "Come on, man! Did you apologize?"

Kevon was now shaking with giggles.

"How am I supposed to do that when I don't think I have anything to apologize for," I said.

"Man, you married? I'm married, right? Sometimes we just gotta apologize for some shit we didn't even do!" Andre finished this bit of wisdom off with an exaggerated shrug. Now Kevon was laughing hysterically.

"I just don't think I can do that," I said. I really couldn't and I'm not even sure it was pride stopping me. In short, it would have felt like a scam. Maybe I apologize and grovel before Kevin and maybe it even mends fences. Then what? I'd be writing articles to his liking for a while, in a morally, ethically, and occupationally dubious rebrand?

All the while, I'd be gathering string for the book you're currently reading, a book I wanted to be as honest as possible about certain events involving one Kevin Durant. How was I to apologize to this guy, only to then go and write this book? Either I'd betray him or the reader. No two ways about that.

Andre and I were at an impasse, much as I hated to disappoint the peacemaker. Andre wasn't finished with his pitch, though. He was about to surprise me.

"Come on, man. Whose career is gonna last longer? Between the two of them?"

"Wait! What?" I stammered.

"Come on. Whose career is gonna last longer?" My read was that Andre was insinuating that he knew my sourcing. Sometimes players do this just to cut the bullshit and other times to prompt a confession. Once, on the road in Brooklyn, a player told me that I'd do better in the locker room if I gave up "who snitched" for an article I'd written. When I said that nobody would trust me, he responded, "A lot of people *in here* would trust you more if you told us." It was a test, I decided. Maybe he was trying to play me. His loyalty was ultimately to his teammates, not to my career or self-conception.

I don't think Andre was trying to play me. He wasn't demanding answers. He was somewhere between giving me shit and trying to help a situation, that in-between space he so often inhabits with everyone, all the time. All I could really do was provide a joke answer to his question.

"Who? KD or my wife?"

Andre let out another exasperated sigh. He turned to Loon. "Some motherfuckers too stupid to help!" He turned back to me and clapped his hands. "Ethan! Get the fuck out!"

Some players were clearly amused by this situation. From what I could gather, KD's pregame rebuke had gotten exaggerated into a bigger sort of blowup. Team staffers were asking about it. DeMarcus Cousins slowly walked across the locker room and turned to me. "Man, you got some apologizing to do," he said, shaking his head.

I responded, "How am I supposed to apologize if I don't think I did anything wrong?"

Boogie shook his head again, then laughed. "Shit. That's for *you* to figure out, man."

In their world, this was how you handled Kevin. He had the power and needed placation. If he was mad, you apologized, even

if you weren't sure about being in the wrong. This is the NBA and might makes right. KD is a superstar and his opinions are worth more than his teammates'. Grate on him and you'll end up on another roster.

For me, it was difficult to see how placating KD would matter in real terms, much as I missed feeling more casual when entering the locker room. As uncomfortable as KD's press conference tirade was, it'd only made me more famous, insofar as I even am. His hatred was commodifiable, not that I asked for it. His forgiveness might have uses, but it was never necessary for getting an exclusive window into the world. The man was such an open wound, telling everyone everything all the time.

Still, one had to be fair. Easy as it was to dislike Durant's tiresome bellyaching, the man had faced incredible trials and tribulations growing up and beyond. Life did not get easier in 2019. On March 21, 2019, Clifford Dixon, a friend of Durant, showed up to his own birthday party at the SL Lounge in Atlanta. Dixon was standing in the parking lot outside the club when he was shot and killed by an assailant who fled the scene. Dixon had been described as an "adopted brother," someone Durant's mother had taken into their home when KD was sixteen years old. For Durant, the tragedy was a heavy burden. For observers, a reminder that Durant's morose ways did not exist in a vacuum.

Many media people did not quite know how to broach it, but KD had lived a particularly difficult life, even for an athlete who'd grown up in poverty, as a few NBA players do. Marcus Thompson, who wrote *KD: Kevin Durant's Relentless Pursuit to Be the Greatest*, said of Durant, in an interview with Colin Cowherd, "He's a kid who grew up in a really rough situation. He never really had the foundation. His life was so unsettled, so I think he's still finding that. He's still looking for that." Sometimes searchers are

pioneering explorers, but oftentimes, they're mostly looking for something they've always lacked.

Describing such matters did not necessarily violate the Old Media Code, yet it was fraught territory to be sure. A famous person's past is often necessary context for understanding them. At the same time, it's easy to talk yourself out of certain strains of storytelling. "It's just sports" is the quick rationalization to leave out details that carry a certain gravity.

When I asked the ever-genial Royce Young, current ESPN reporter and founder of the *Daily Thunder* blog, about whether he'd elided anything meaningful from his coverage of KD, Young replied, "I think some of the stuff about his family life, but I don't know if that was fair. I think it's a really important thing about him, but I don't know if it's fair game."

As a media collective, we were all too happy to talk about Kevin Durant's family when he delivered a powerhouse MVP speech in 2014 as a member of the Thunder. The speech, mostly written by Thunder PR man Matt Tumbleson, included a memorable acknowledgment of Durant's mother. With tears in his eyes, and his voice cracking, Durant told his mom, "You the real MVP."

It wasn't the first time fans both in and outside Oklahoma connected with Durant over that maternal bond. One of the lasting images of KD's career came out of the Thunder losing to LeBron's Heat, in the 2012 NBA Finals. The ABC camera followed KD down the hall of the American Airlines Arena, where he paused, and with tears in his eyes, gave a lengthy hug to his mother and father, Wayne. KD's pain and his salve was on display for the world to see. It was just as TV producers want pain processed and distributed to the masses: a situation that almost nobody can relate to (Disappointed as an NBA superstar) was packaged as something billions can relate to (Relying on parental comfort in our painful moments).

Wanda Pratt Durant was a courtside fixture at Thunder games, often shown on camera. She was effervescent as parent cheerleader, swinging a towel in the air in rhythm with the crowd. "Mama Durant" was as much a part of the Thunder brand as anyone in the organization. This wasn't just a small-town team that preached the virtues of "family." Literal family was part of the journey fans were connecting to.

It was different in Oakland. Wanda was seen in the first season, but not so much in the following ones. Warriors coaches, staffers, players, and media started to note the absence. Where was she? What happened to her? She was present alongside KD at the opening of the Durant Center in Prince George's County on January 22, 2019. Other than that, Wanda was scarce.

"Yeah, I don't think their relationship's in a good place, but that's standard for the Durant world," Young explained, back in spring of 2019. "It's somebody's in, somebody's out. Feuding with this person, not happy with this person, then they make up. Then they come back. That was the experience in Oklahoma City, constantly."

In the aftermath of KD's departure from Golden State, Mama Durant returned to his life. A *Wall Street Journal* profile on Durant's journey to the Brooklyn Nets mentioned Wanda Pratt's role in helping Durant postsurgery:

> She then followed him to a suite at the Four Seasons, where she did all the things he couldn't do for himself. "He was in the tub," Wanda says, "and I was washing him, and we were talking, making sure his leg didn't get wet and the bandage stayed dry, and he said: 'Mom, it feels good to have you take care of me.' And it just—"
>
> She stops, overcome with emotion. The moment was especially sweet because not long ago mother and son were on the outs.

Wanda had been handling Durant's financial affairs since he broke into the league, but in 2014 he decided to take control. It caused a rift, which took months, Durant says, to heal.

In KD's saga from Oklahoma City to Oakland and on to Brooklyn, Rich Kleiman was the constant. The former music agent, who shared a matching tattoo with Durant, was thought to have the greatest influence on him. Rich was, in many ways, the kind of person people imagine when they think "agent." Bald, tall, adorned with a large Star of David diamond chain, Rich was an extroverted gabber, schmoozing his way from the family room to courtside and back, every game. Though he came off like an easygoing former frat guy, Rich was believed to have attained a Svengali strain of influence. If the Warriors were a palace, Kleiman was its Rasputin.

When the "KD to the Knicks" rumors started, many in the league assumed it was part of a deal to elevate Rich. The Knicks were his childhood team and New York was his base of operations. It was announced, midway in the 2018–2019 season, that Thirty Five Ventures, Durant's entertainment company, was moving its offices to New York. At this point, it appeared that only conflict within KD's inner circle could save the Warriors. They were about to lose the man they'd wooed from Oklahoma City, if he wasn't gone already.

Everything changes in the NBA, but most everything that happens has happened before in some incarnation. There's an article on Rick Barry's alienation from the April 25, 1983, *Sports Illustrated* titled "A Voice Crying Out in the Wilderness." In it, Tony Kornheiser—yes, *that* Tony Kornheiser of *Pardon the Interruption* fame—chronicles the postretirement ennui of a less than lovable Warriors superstar who never got his due.

"Barry wanted fame and all that went with it," Kornheiser wrote. "He wore his talent like a crown and his attitude like a target. In the world according to Barry, winning was everything. And the way to win was to put the ball in his hands. If a great pass was needed, he would make it. If a last-second shot was needed, he would take it. His team would win, and he would be the hero. Everyone would know that they couldn't have done it without him. How could you begrudge him glory when he delivered? What more could you want?"

"What more could you want?" seems to be a theme for Kevin as well, when he's grousing. He does what we want and we still hate.

Kornheiser quoted former star Tom Meschery, in an aside that cuts to the bone.

"All former professional athletes, not just Barry, are victims," Meschery says. "But Rick may be more victimized than the rest of us who weren't quite so good. It's a terribly difficult transition from that world to this. Not so much in giving up the sport as in giving up the idea of oneself. You had come to see yourself as larger than life. Rick was so hungry for fame that when he got it, it was easy for him to get lost in it. He was so caught up in image that he probably lost sight of himself. People were eager to make allowances for everything he did, and so there was never any reason for him to stop doing them. He was constantly told—so naturally he came to believe—that life on a pedestal was reality."

The article closed on a since retired, depressive Barry retelling a recurring dream. It was the kind of dream a kid might have, shooting hoops in his driveway: the crowd roaring, willing him forward, until he dunks over Julius Erving, sending his team to victory. As Kornheiser wrote:

"It feels so great, so wonderful," he says. "I hear them cheering for me."

Cheering just for him.

"And the best thing is," Barry says, "that they're not just cheering for me because I won the game. They're cheering for me because they like me. In my dream, the thing that's different is that they really like me."

No matter what Kevin Durant did, no matter how great his play, this would never be the payoff. These strangers would never love him for him.

On March 2, 2019, sports media impresario Bill Simmons conducted a news-making one-on-one panel with NBA commissioner Adam Silver at the MIT Sloan Sports Analytics Conference. Though Simmons is by nature loquacious, the conversation was dominated by the usually circumspect Silver. The commissioner had things on his mind, perhaps principally, that his game's biggest stars were alienated and depressed. It's rare to hear a commissioner speak like this, as commissioners are, in effect, PR officials for their respective leagues. The issues Silver broached had apparently metastasized to the point where there was simply no hiding it any longer.

When Simmons asked about player happiness and its impact on free agency, Silver responded, "One is a larger societal issue and I know you have a lot of young people who work for you at The Ringer. Obviously our players are young, we have young people in our office. I think we live a bit in the age of anxiety. I've read studies on this. I think part of it is a direct product of social media. I think those players we're talking about, when I meet with them, what strikes me is that they are truly unhappy." The placid commissioner's eyes bulged a bit and his eyebrows bobbled on "truly unhappy." There was an urgency in his tone.

"This is not some show that they're putting on for the media, when I'm one on one with a lot of these guys I think, to the outside world, they see the fame, the money, all the trappings that go with it. They're the best in the world at what they do. They say, 'How is it possible they could even be complaining?' I hear this on television all the time. A lot of these young men are genuinely unhappy. Some have come from very difficult circumstances, that doesn't help. Some of them are amazingly isolated and you and I have talked about this."

Silver then referenced an upcoming documentary on Michael Jordan's last season with the Bulls, in which he saw a level of camaraderie currently absent from the spot.

"I mean the camaraderie was incredible. I mean, Michael, what people didn't see was that he and Phil Jackson obviously as the coach deserves enormous credit. There was classic team building going on all the time. These guys were a band of brothers on the buses, on the planes, and all the attention only brought them closer. If you're around a team this day and age, [they have their] headphones on, and they're isolated and they're head down. It used to be, Isaiah Thomas said to me, 'Championships are won on the bus.'"

Were championships not won on the bus anymore? Or were they only won at the pitch meeting? It was hard to even contemplate such questions in the immediate aftermath of Silver napalming his own league.

This was a radical change in tone from previous years—hell, decades—of NBA commish speak. Basketball might not have been America's favorite sport, but the NBA always could console itself with being the most "with it" sport. Sure, the NFL was bigger and baseball made more money. But the NBA was relevant. It was cool. It was young. The future would be theirs because they were so uniquely wired into the upcoming generation's present.

In an August 20, 2018, podcast with *HoopsHype*, Twitter CEO Jack Dorsey spoke glowingly about "NBA Twitter," a nexus of players, teams, media, and fans in constant, lively conversation on the platform. Dorsey attributed its growth to the NBA's intent.

"I think NBA Twitter, I think the first reason's it's become strong is the league's acceptance of it," Dorsey said. "Not just acceptance but usage of it. There's a very open mindset to technologies like Twitter and I think that's helped immensely. . . . We were fortunate to get a lot of the players onto the service and a lot of the commentators and the smart commentators."

For years, most stories about the NBA and social media were glowingly positive, a tale of stunning industry success. From a May 31, 2018, *Washington Post* story on the NBA's conquest of social media:

> It's no accident that the NBA has cultivated a devoted online following. The league has leveraged social media to stay relevant, to keep its fans—especially those who skew younger and more tech-savvy—engaged year-round.
>
> "If I knew what the secret sauce was, I'd bottle it up and spread it around to every single league property that I work with," said TJ Adeshola, Twitter's head of sports league partnerships. "NBA Twitter just has this really special connectivity to it that doesn't exist anywhere else. It's really reflective of the league's approach in the broader marketplace to be innovative, to give their players this level of authenticity and connectivity. It's relatively unprecedented in the sports space, which lends itself to a perfect, perfect marriage with a Twitter platform. The league has been the one to lift up the hood and give folks a unique view."

The NFL, mired for years in poor publicity, was tweaked for not being like its younger, cooler little brother. Almost nobody was

asking whether this was all headed in a positive direction, or whether so much connectivity might have downsides. The future was bright, and most importantly, for the sake of selling a game, the future was fun. As the *Post* article framed it, "On social media, there's nothing like NBA Twitter. It's a sports bar that doesn't close, a barbershop with unlimited seating, a family cookout where the NBA stars show up to hang." Everyone was having a good time, it seemed.

On October 1, 2018, Bleacher Report posted an article by Tom Haberstroh titled "Is Social Media Addiction in the NBA Out of Control?" Haberstroh interviewed shooting guard JJ Redick on his decision to delete social media applications. "It's a dark place," Redick said of social media. "It's not a healthy place. It's not real. It's not a healthy place for ego if we're talking about some Freudian shit. It's just this cycle of anger and validation and tribalism. It's scary, man."

Phones had become a problem in matters spiritual and practical. Teams were struggling to communicate with players whose heads were always tilted down. Haberstroh's article details a coach desperately seeking outside help to curb his team's habits.

When he arrived, he sat down with a behavior designer named Matthew Mayberry from Boundless Mind, an artificial-intelligence startup that works out of a one-car garage. The 10-employee tech company, launched by T. Dalton Combs and Ramsay Brown under its previous name Dopamine Labs, has been featured on a *60 Minutes* report called "Brain Hacking" because of what its team of neuroscientists is working on. The coach and Mayberry talked about his team and, specifically, the phone addiction that had overtaken the locker room.

"How do I get players and staff to put down their damn phones in meetings?" the coach asked. "Can we turn phone addiction away from time sucks like Instagram and Twitter and

toward productive tasks like watching film or studying scouting reports? Can we actually change these habits?"

Teams have tried certain reforms, "phone buckets" and "phone bags" during team meals, for instance. These attempts might be beneficial, but overall, there's no wrenching back the clock's hands to a more sane era. Throwing one phone in a bucket doesn't change the reality of an entire society operating via phones. Even if players eschew social media for all the right reasons, it will still find a way to creep into their lives and cause complications.

At the 2019 All-Star Weekend in Charlotte, KD and Kyrie were frequently spotted together. Given season-long rumors attaching the two to a New York Knicks future, these scenes fed into a certain theme that weekend. Reporter Ben Stinar tweeted out a clip of KD and Kyrie backstage of the game, in animated, friendly dialogue. It was a mundane clip at first glance, perhaps until the Basketball Forever Twitter account layered some interpretation onto the images. The site's tweet read, "Kyrie Irving has been caught on video saying, 'two max slots, it's time' to Kevin Durant."

The popular assumption based off this reading: Kyrie and KD were conversing about how the Knicks had opened up cap space for two max-level superstars and that it was time to join up. There's no way to prove whether this lip reading and interpretation was correct, but that did not prevent the clip from going viral.

When Irving was asked about the viral video, he was understandably less than pleased. From the *Boston Globe* article by Nicole Yang:

"It's my life, right?" Irving said. "It's two people talking, having a conversation. If this was the real world, would it be anybody else's business? It's a video of somebody assuming what we're talking about, making an opinion about it, right? So, why would I care

about it? Why does it have an impact on my life? Why are you asking me those type of questions?"

The 26-year-old proceeded to go back and forth with a re-porter, arguing the intent behind the incessant questioning was for "the likes and clicks."

It's easy to empathize with Kyrie Irving's displeasure. He was being spied on, his secrets stolen and used by strangers toward ends that further complicate his life. This is indeed a crazy way to live. No individual is solely at fault for Kyrie's travails, and that might be another frustrating aspect of living inside The Take Zone. There's nobody to blame. It's just the hive mind and its minions, doing what comes naturally. You are always being watched and recorded by anonymous informants. When they find what they crave, your business will become everyone's business and you will have no specific enemy to fault for that.

When the *Boston Globe* reporter told Irving that the fans were interested in his private conversation, Kyrie responded, "Oh the fans? This is about the fans? So you write for the fans?"

Ah yes, the fans. Those people. Kyrie's mordant "So you write for the fans?" is revealing in a way. Few in this highly cynical league could envision a person actually, deeply caring about "the fans."

Even if the fans were often thanked at public team events and retirement ceremonies, their existence is mostly just tolerated at this point. The paying customers are just so rarely part of con-versations within the league, away from the microphones. There are many reasons for this, but one in particular is that their love looks ghoulish and horrifying from the recipient's vantage. Walk behind Steph Curry as he walks past the seats above the locker room tunnel, and you see animalistic hysteria. People are shoving one another and grasping in spasms. They are shrieking like the possessed. Their faces are contorted. If this is what fan love looks

like up close, then how sick must hatred look? You couldn't blame a player for believing that it's all the same thing.

Online can be so much worse. There, players and media experience depravity that you might not ever find in prison. This isn't most fans, but the scorn is just more notable. When we feel attacked and that fight-or-flight drive kicks in, we tend to remember the experience. I often hear from media members about how awful the fans on Twitter are. I'll take a glance at their mentions and often see mostly anodyne or positive responses. Those don't stick, apparently.

Steve Kerr tells a story about getting on Twitter for the first time as a broadcaster. The first reply he read complimented him on how he called the game that night. "I'm like, 'Yeah, I *did* do a good job,'" Steve recalls, grinning and making a fist pump. The next response was similar. More grinning, more happy. "This is pretty awesome," Steve says. The third response was not so complimentary. "Hey Steve," the tweet read. "How about you get LeBron's cock out of your mouth." Kerr remembers flashing into anger, muttering something like, "Fuck you, motherfucker." In that moment, he grasped the absurdity of the situation. He had allowed two strangers to lift his spirits up in the air and another to send them hurtling earthward. "What am I doing?!" Kerr said, shaking his head in amazement at himself.

The asymmetrical power of insults can eventually taint your view of your customers. If "the fans" are most easily accessed on a medium that sometimes pumps out these memorable insults, it can be easy to conflate "the fans" with toxicity. On social media, the power of the asshole fan is disproportionate. Many NBA types wish to drink from the cool fountain of compliments. The problem is, if 5 percent of the water is sulfuric acid, then the clean 95 percent hardly matters. Currently, there's no easy solution to this problem beyond "Stop reading the responses."

And so the fans are either resented or banished from mind. Sometimes, it's as though players, coaches, and media wish to forge an alternate reality where this sport is serious and edifying enough to stand alone. This is, of course, absurd. Back in 2014, Steph Curry asked me why there was such media momentum behind making Clippers-Warriors a rivalry. "Why does it have to be a rivalry?" he said. "What's the point?" New and stupid about the job, but still having had more time than Steph to contemplate the silliness of it, I responded, "It's what the people want. What's the point throwing a sphere at a ring? What's the point of anything?" PR man Raymond Ridder wearily interjected, "Oh God. I guess we can all go home now."

Fans are the reason any of this ridiculous sphere-through-ring sport can be a profession, but few in the sport are keen on expressing any gratitude for that, at least in private. For one, nobody likes the fan who expresses entitled rage by saying, "I pay your salary!" Secondly, why would players express gratitude when, as Adam Silver notes, they're so manifestly unhappy?

Over the 2018–2019 season, Durant was certainly among the unhappy. By midseason, KD had drifted, save for unpredictable flickers of being present. There were points in film sessions where he'd look down at his shoes, responding to nothing as Kerr tried to speak to him. "Sometimes he'd have input," said someone who was in those sessions. "It was strange. Some days he'd have really good input, and everyone was kind of shocked. And then he might not say anything for six straight film sessions. His personality went up and down like a yo-yo." During time-outs, Durant would wrap his face in a towel, under his hoodie. Looking something between a *Mortal Kombat* character and a mummy, KD would drift away from his teammates' huddle all the way to the basket stanchion, where he'd stand alone.

There have been Different Dudes in the NBA before and there have been egos to manage. What made this situation unique was the effort and care teammates put into reeling Durant back in over the course of the season. The combination of KD's immense talent and palpable distress made for a situation that teammates wished to mitigate. "Usually guys are like 'fuck you' if you don't want to buy in," one player explained. "We have to force hello out of you every day? But because of who he is and how good he is, guys really tried."

Two weeks after the viral All-Star Weekend video, Kyrie and his Celtics came to Oracle Arena for a nationally televised game. The Warriors were crushed by 33 points in one of KD's worst games of the season.

On what the Warriors lacked that evening, Kerr told media, "It starts with a passion, and an anger and an intensity, and it wasn't there tonight."

Durant took the podium, wearing his White Sox Hat of Talismanic Defiance. When told of Kerr's "anger" comment, KD was scornful. "I thought we move off of joy?" Durant asked, referencing a phrase Kerr frequently employs to characterize the Warriors' style of play. "Now it's anger? Okay. I disagree with that one. I think all around, top to bottom, coaches, players, we just gotta be better."

Beyond Durant taking the ever-controversial anti-joy position, this was the continuation of a trend that had been building. KD was taking shots at Kerr in postgame press conferences, sometimes veiled, other times obvious.

Why was he taking shots? Beyond his specific disagreements with Kerr's choices, Durant was just less than happy, outwardly, even on the days he wasn't yelling at reporters for being improper happiness arbiters. There's a more subversive idea attached to KD's sarcastic mocking of joy, if we try to empathize. What if he's right to mock the idea? What if happiness has nothing to do with whether a team wins or loses?

Kerr would certainly disagree with that formulation. When the Bulls swept Shaquille O'Neal's hypertalented Orlando Magic team, Kerr claims he saw it coming. "They weren't together," he recalled of the series. In Kerr's view, a certain esprit de corps is necessary for ultimate success. Shaq and costar Penny Hardaway were at odds, feuding over matters of ego, with Shaq even taking a shot at Penny's Nike ads in a Reebok ad of his own.

It's an open question as to how much happiness matters in sports. It's clear that we wish it mattered. Watch almost any sports movie and you'll see a contented team coming together spiritually, concurrent with a montage of win after win.

Reality might be different. Our memories have a tendency to play tricks. The team that won had chemistry. The team that lost would have had chemistry, if only a shot or two fell. We want chemistry to be real, and we see it even when it's not there or can't be known either way.

Tom Haberstroh told me a story that stuck, from his days covering the Big Three Miami Heat. The Heat were a highly functional squad, winning two championships and playing in four Finals over the course of their famously scrutinized four-year run. Tom had assumed the Heat were a fairly together unit, given their accomplishments and what they conveyed to the media. LeBron's surprise exit off to Cleveland revealed fissures that had been long hidden. Suddenly, players and coaches were freer to discuss long-simmering feuds. Tom got a sense of which players disliked Heat coach Erik Spoelstra and which players resented one another. There was no reason to maintain the veneer any longer.

We may never know how much playing with joy matters, just as we may never know exactly what makes Kevin Durant happy, but what's clear is the following: happiness matters for keeping everybody in one place. Maybe Kerr is wrong about why the Orlando Magic got swept in 1996, but he's not wrong that they

were falling apart as a team. Shaq preferred movie-star ambitions to his Orlando teammates and went west that summer. Shaq and Kobe were an all-time duo that couldn't stand one another's company enough to keep leveraging their tandem advantage over everyone else. The Warriors had the most talent for KD to play alongside and some good years remaining. Still, he had a foot out the door because that setup wasn't satiating emotionally.

Joy might not be the reason for victory, but it sustains the will to maintain a victorious operation. When the happiness ebbs, it's time for players to go their separate ways, to chase individual aspirations in new locations. Joy is perhaps less the fuel and more the glue of greatness.

Whatever joy's utility, by the middle of the 2019 season, Kevin Durant's joy seemed to have run out.

6

THE FINAL MARCH AFTER APRIL

The joy may have dissipated, but the will to fight out-
lived happiness and maybe even fulfillment. The ground-level
competitors never stopped competing. In the end though, that fire
could not survive fate. Everything comes to an end.

A week after the 2019 NBA Finals ended, I was with my wife
and toddler at Creekwood, a modern Italian establishment on the
Oakland-Berkeley border. Over the restaurant chatter, I heard
a familiar voice cutting through and informing waiters that her
husband was parking and on his way. I looked up and saw Leah
Adams, ever-amiable wife of Warrior assistant coach Ron Adams,
legendary connoisseur of Italian eateries. Leah, charmingly bois-
terous as a default mode, has always seemed the perfect contrast
to the normally placid Ron. Upon seeing me, she did not even
pause to say, "Hello." Instead she exclaimed, "Have you ever seen a
season end worse than ours?!"

I couldn't come up with a counterpoint and the question lingered in the air. Ron arrived, and my smiling son waddled up to

the couple. "He's got such a great disposition," Ron appraised, before turning to me. "He's so positive. Why can't you be more like him?"

Maybe Ron had a point. Maybe I should defy convention, break with Leah, and appreciate how the 2019 Finals didn't end so badly. The outcome of the 2016 Finals left the Warriors with much pain and regret. If only Draymond Green hadn't punched LeBron James in the dick. If only Steph Curry had played smarter. If only Steve Kerr hadn't subbed in Festus Ezeli. If only. And so, in 2016, there were tears in the locker room. In 2019, there was a head shake here and a head shake there. Overall, there was a stoic acceptance of fate, plus some scoffing at the ultimate manifestation of the "when it rains, it pours" absurdity.

To lose the 2019 Finals seemed like losing to nature. Kevin Durant blew out his Achilles in Game 5 and Klay Thompson tore his ACL in Game 6. The Warriors may have their internal recriminations regarding how Durant's medical situation was handled, but the outcome itself? They had fought hard, gotten hurt, and lost. It was a disaster of the highest order, a spectacularly cruel and gruesome end. It just wasn't one that fell on the players, the main protagonists in the eyes of fans.

The playoffs were supposed to be a malaise ender for the Warriors, after so much time spent slogging through meaningless regular-season games. They'd won the games they needed to win during those first six months, and now, finally, meaning had arrived. Not only would the Warriors win the championship, but they would do so with a purpose absent in so many of their shaky Oracle performances. Kevin Durant had been playing oddly down the regular season stretch, not shooting when open and hot-potatoing the ball. Kerr would praise the play in his press conferences, but everyone within and around the team knew the truth: this was not the preferred modality.

KD had been so dominant in the playoffs before, so the hope was that its arrival would wake Kevin up. This speaks to what a brilliant and bizarre player Kevin Durant is. There was little concern of Kevin choking on the big stage—just an expectation that he might finally be motivated enough to fully access his copious talent, through the fog of misery.

The Warriors hosted the Clippers in their last regular-season game at Oracle Arena, on April 7. While the Clips had many of their players sitting, one starter managed to make a kind of impact from the bench. In the second quarter, Steph Curry was fouled hard and set up to shoot a couple free throws. The crowd, as it often does, showered their favorite player with a full-throated, "M-V-P" chant. This did not escape the notice of starting Clipper point guard and habitual nuisance Patrick Beverley. "See," Beverley said to KD from the Clipper bench. "They don't want you." The two would get into it along the sideline later on. Beverley was poking a wound.

A week later, the Clippers returned to Oakland for the first round of the playoffs. The forty-eight-win Clips had done just enough to make the postseason, and were widely assumed to be roadkill in this series. Doc Rivers's team had tremendously exceeded expectations in a rebuilding year. Just making the playoffs was enough.

So the Clippers played like a team with little to lose and deployed their novel strategy: Patrick Beverley, merely six feet tall in socks, was to be Kevin Durant's primary defender. The visual was absurd, and the results were initially suboptimal in Game 1. When the Clippers sent help defenders over, KD easily passed over Beverley's head. Still, Beverley kept the pressure on, crowding him, barking at him, mocking him with an exaggerated flop gesticulation.

Beverley wasn't the main source of frustration for the Warriors, though. In a two-hour film session, it had been stressed to

DeMarcus Cousins that he must do a dribble handoff for the Warriors' elite shooters when left open. Given that he shot 28 percent from deep that season, on mostly wide-open shots, the Clippers were happy to concede these attempts.

The problem was that Cousins was still happy to shoot. He appeared to take his instructions as an affront, jacking twelve times in twenty-one minutes and making only four attempts. The DeMarcus signing had not gone exactly as planned. In theory, he was supposed to make this roster historically great, an intimidating "Five All-Stars" unit, the likes of which the basketball world had never seen. Joe Lacob was especially proud of the signing. Cousins had come to them, for a mere midlevel exception, and the league had quaked in fear and jealous rage.

In practice, it had been difficult rehabbing Cousins, coming off an Achilles tear, back into live action. Perhaps a happier Warriors team could have inculcated Cuz into the ways of its culture, but this wasn't an especially joyous or focused moment in the Warrior timeline. Cousins, after many years spent playing for bad, dysfunctional teams in Sacramento and New Orleans, was now a part of greatness. But greatness wasn't the promised paradise. Greatness meant less impetus for winning regular-season games and that feuds between players were national news. Before rehabbing his way back onto the court, Cousins's highest-profile cameo was as attempted peacemaker in the November 12, 2018, KD-Draymond feud.

Still, the incentives were aligned for DeMarcus to do what the Warriors needed. When it comes to player acquisition, teams often think in terms of incentives. They don't trust every player to try their best, all the time. The men of Ops tend to place more faith in monetary motivation.

It would be nice if every player were self-motivated, but GMs and coaches know better. They anticipate the drop-off that follows

a secured contract. With Cousins, the hope was that he would be a perfect citizen because his money depended on it. He had just struggled to get a payday and had chosen the Warriors to rehab his status. If he were an out-of-shape handful on a championship roster, teams would shun him.

Cousins and the Warriors might have had a different conception of what rehabbing an image means. To the Warriors, if Cousins merely executed game plans, they would win, interested teams would call them up, and they would tell them of Cousins's great citizenship. Money would flow into Cousins's coffers.

DeMarcus's perspective might have been different, and he wouldn't be crazy to see it differently. Former backup big JaVale McGee had rehabilitated his image with the Warriors and won two championships while scoring efficiently in minor minutes. No big payday followed. Of course, JaVale was widely known within the league as a bit of a goofball, but there wasn't much evidence that performing like an adequate role player did much beyond earning plaudits internally. And so Cousins kept jacking up his shots, at least until he suffered a serious quad injury in his second-ever playoff game.

With all this going on, the Warriors were collectively off. On the Warriors' first play of Game 2, slight rookie Landry Shamet was defensively switched onto KD, an advantageous matchup for Durant. With a clear path into the lane, KD instead shifted his weight backward and tossed a soft pass into the clutches of another Clipper rookie, Shai Gilgeous-Alexander. Durant was floating, meandering about the floor and passing without much purpose.

In the second quarter, Kerr and Durant were seen jawing at one another, midpossession. It's one thing to see it happen on the bench, but rarer to see it during the course of play. Kerr was heard telling KD to be more aggressive. KD was yelling back that he knew how to play and not to tell him anything. At 3:04 left in

the third quarter, KD set up to shoot a couple free throws. The crowd mounted a modest "M-V-P" chant. Evidently unimpressed or disbelieving, KD smirked and repeatedly shook his head. Upon making the second free throw he backpedaled while waving off the crowd with a bat of his hand.

"Is that fair for fans to cheer for two MVPs on the same team?" mused Chris Webber on the TNT broadcast. "Shouldn't you have to pick one?" Veteran play-by-play man Marv Albert replied, "I heard, actually, a faint chant for Durant." Neither appeared to notice Durant's reaction, or if they did, made no mention. According to a Warriors staffer within earshot, Durant said to the crowd, "Oh *now* you love me, huh?" The Warriors would go on to blow a 31-point lead and lose.

After the game, Kerr was asked about KD's performance. "He had a tough night," he said tersely. During Kerr's press conference, Durant was exiting Oracle. Despite league rules requiring players to be available for comment after playoff games, KD was skipping, leaving Steph and company to answer the hard questions.

The next practice was quite eventful. Kerr spoke to media first and answered questions about Durant's lackluster performance. "The guy is the most skilled basketball player on planet earth," Kerr said. "There's nobody who can do what he can do. It's the playoffs. Defenses are more locked in. They play everybody tougher. I don't know how many shots he got the other night. Seven? Eight? Absolutely, he needs to be more aggressive. It's the playoffs. He can get any shot he wants, any time. So I want to see him get twenty shots. Thirty."

Normally players enjoy having carte blanche to launch, but KD took this suggestion in a different way. When informed of Kerr's comments Durant told media, "I'm not going to go out there and just shoot twenty, thirty shots. I don't play like that. We were up thirty points and I had five shots. Everybody's shots

were evenly distributed around that time, when we were up thirty. So me taking two more shots after that wasn't the reason why we lost."

Mark Medina of the Bay Area News Group asked, "How about the aggression part of it?"

Durant shot back, "Tell me how you want me to play."

Medina gently responded, "I'm just asking for your perspective."

Durant said, "I just want to have a conversation on how you feel I should play."

When Medina responded that it wasn't for him to decide, Durant unleashed a dissertation on why he wasn't scoring on a much smaller man.

"When I get the ball in my positions to score, I would look to score. If I don't have the option to score, I'll look to pass. We run a lot of plays here, we move the ball down court. Every time I touch it, I'm not going to break the play just to be aggressive just because I need to get up thirty shots because it looks like something's wrong with me. Nah. I'm going to play basketball. We won Game 1 that way, we were up thirty in Game 2. I think we need to stick to the game plan we had the first three-and-a-half quarters and do that for forty-eight minutes."

KD was then asked if he broke down film like a coach. He was animated in response.

"Yep, I do break it down. Well, we had a nice flow of the game. Let's go back to the whole last month of the season. We've been playing this way for a while. When we got into this series, Game 1, we had some nice momentum. They're playing a gimmick defense, which has been working, top-locking everything on the perimeter, so guys aren't even looking at the three-point line, they're just forcing guys inside the three-point line. So, for us, when I get the ball in my spots, I got a pest, Patrick Beverley, who is up underneath me. Well, I could definitely shoot up over the

top and score every time if it's a one-on-one situation. But we got a guy who is dropping and helping. Then we got another guy that's just sitting on me waiting for me to dribble the basketball. If I put the basketball on the floor, I could probably make forty-three percent of my shots if I shoot them like that. But that's not really going to do nothing for us with the outcome of the game. Because we got a nice flow, everybody touching the rock, everybody shooting and scoring. I'm not going to get in the way of the game because I want to have a little back-and-forth with Patrick Beverley."

Then the monologue reached a crescendo point as KD surveyed the media crowd: "I'm Kevin Durant. You know who I am. Y'all know who I am." His last words in the press conference were, "I know y'all want to talk to me for the rest of the day because I got so much knowledge. But I gotta go."

Many in media loved Durant's analysis. Multiple writers called the explanation "insightful." Finally, basketball analysis from an athlete! Durant, who was rarely savvy at PR, had done something reputation-positive here. This treatise hit the right notes for the basketball intelligentsia. "I could probably make forty-three percent of my shots if I shoot them like that" played into an analytics-friendly eschewing of "hero ball," the less efficient basketball machismo popularized by Kobe Bryant. A generation of NBA stars came to believe in the value of shooting contested midrange jumpers. A generation of basketball nerds came to believe that these jocks needed to understand how stupid this was. KD's rejection of "forty three-percent" flattered nerd sensibilities.

Never mind that the Clippers had zero rim protection and weren't throwing an inordinate amount of help at Durant. Never mind that KD was, again, taking to the stage and undermining his coach's message. Never mind that there was little strategy in tossing away nine turnovers and jogging back in transition whenever he coughed them up.

In short, Durant wasn't giving a great effort. In another era, I think we'd just say what was obvious. Taboos had crept into the industry over time, though not always for the worse. In the past, sportswriter assessments of athletes could more often be cartoonishly uninformed if not transparently racist. Also, the media culture had just gotten more self-aware, probably because you were far more likely to hear and read negative things about yourself in the social media age. We knew we were nerds critiquing jocks. We knew it looked ridiculous prima facie. We were speaking with a moral authority that we ourselves hardly believed in. So, nobody could just say, "He's out there not trying."

As a nerd, I agreed in spirit on eschewing stupid, selfish shots, but Durant's framing was false. There were efficient options to be had. Moreover, the opinion was hardly my own. The Warriors coaches had little patience for what KD was selling to the media. Whatever the result in Game 2, Durant's actions were confirming some of their worst fears. He was detaching. At best, he would be totally unpredictable going forward. At worst, he would be checked out.

For a couple of days, KD was a central topic of sports talk discussion. "I'm Kevin Durant. You know who I am" set up a series in which we'd all be keen to see some greater truth of identity revealed. Was he disengaging? Had he already quit on the Warriors?

Staples Center is always a scene, not just because it's a celebrity playground, but also because Los Angeles is where the majority of NBA agents and managers reside. As I walked around the court in pregame, I could see LeBron's manager and best friend, Maverick Carter, sitting beside Rich Kleiman. On the court, during Durant's warmups, Jerry West, now with the Clippers, took KD aside and whispered something into his ear. "That's good for us!" a couple Clipper fans seated behind me exclaimed, giddily. The Clips were overmatched, but this is all merely a showcase. They

were free agent players, on the make. They were playing with house money, having already exceeded expectations by merely making the postseason. The Clips had plenty of cap space and assets accrued in trades. They were also the rumored free agency destination of Kawhi Leonard, a rumor that had the virtue of actually coming true.

The Clippers were an ambitious operation, run by big-spirited macher Steve Ballmer. The former Microsoft CEO is a broad-shouldered six foot five, with a friar's balding pattern and large hands. He doesn't walk about the premises so much as he struts, his head jutted forward at all times. As his leaning dome bobs his large nose forward, he looks a little like if you stuffed a giant bald eagle into a collared shirt. This is an excellent look for a CEO, if slightly terrifying. A sizeable, aggressive balding man is the Fortune 500 prototype.

Steve Ballmer's vigor is well chronicled. There's a YouTube clip titled "Steve Ballmer Going Crazy on Stage," wherein the billionaire jumps around, yelping to the point of accreting massive pit stains. He takes to the mic and yells, "Who said sit down!?" at his employees. Then he tells them, "I have four words. I. Love. This. Company—yeaaaahhhhh!" Ballmer's voice keeps cracking during the shouts.

That was Ballmer in a stale corporate setting. During the passion-inflaming action of an NBA game, he looked something between a man badly in need of an exorcism or porta potty. The cameras loved every bug-eyed shriek, every writhing contortion.

With two hours until Game 3 tip-off, I figured I'd schmooze around the arena event level, next to the Clippers locker room. There were other reporters milling about, people I hadn't seen in some months. Ballmer strolled up to a Clippers employee, who remarked on how much fun it was to see those camera shots of

his in-game reactions. He was particularly ecstatic during Game 2's 31-point comeback, a perfect vehicle for a TV producer to demonstrate the moment's passion. "Ahhh," Ballmer boomed, "I don't like it. I just hate the way it takes away from our players."

I didn't believe him, but that's the right thing to say. Also, think what you will about Ballmer, but he's a presence and the Clippers were improving their station. As Ballmer demurred about his cameos, Clipper big man Montrezl Harrell entered the arena. He walked past us as cameramen backpedaled while keeping him in frame. They didn't have to backpedal too fast because Trez was walking slowly, holding his baby son's hand.

So much of the NBA is artifice, or at the very least, contrivance. These stoic arena entrances had become a fashion runway of sorts, with players now regularly donning outrageous outfits for the TV cameras. The pregame studio will show at least one player slow-trudging into the arena with oversized headphones and a solemn stare. It's now clout to be competed over. ESPN won't show everyone's cool guy entrance to millions. If you're something less than a superstar, you need to go above and beyond for such real estate.

Harrell's outfit was themed and matched to his beautiful baby boy. The child was clearly a bit new to walking, but better practiced at it than my baby at the time. He waddled gingerly, guided by his dad. It was undeniably adorable. Both were wearing green and white, the father sporting a baseball jersey that read "G-Baby" on the back. Montrezl was also wearing a baseball hat that simply read, "Dad." Harrell is likely a wonderful father with an understandable inclination to shout his paternal love from the rooftops, but there was something hilarious about the whole careful spectacle.

It was very NBA. Babies have recently become not just pregame accoutrements but postgame as well. After the final game

of Dwyane Wade's career, Wade sported a red suit with no shirt underneath to his closing press conference. If that wasn't an arresting enough image, he answered questions while holding his baby daughter, outfitted with a matching red jumpsuit and red bow that couldn't contain her wriggling. Fatherhood had actually made me less understanding of this practice than I had been in the past. Back then, I figured it was a parenting thing, something you would finally grasp upon having a child. Now that I had a baby, this display just seemed bizarre and burdensome. When holding my son, sans bottle of formula, the last thing I'd have wanted was to ramp up the degree of difficulty by answering questions while containing his outbursts. But maybe that's the difference between us and athletes. They like a challenge.

During the Warriors' 2015 title run, Steph Curry's daughter Riley, then two years old, became a viral sensation when Steph held her during his press conferences. A few reporters objected and incurred the wrath of Twitter and media-critical websites. Steph was annoyed too, sarcastically referencing the criticism a few times in the locker room back then.

Four years later, he changed his mind on the matter. In a February 2019 interview with *The Undefeated*, Curry said, "I think even as parents, understanding how we're going to raise kids not only in this crazy society we live in but one that we're so visible [in], and people are kind of locked into every step we take, every word we say. One thing I do technically regret in terms of how fast this all came is when I brought Riley on the podium [during the 2015 NBA Finals]."

He added, "I didn't know how much that would blow up and how much of a splash she [would make] on the scene. If I could take that one back, I probably would, just because my goal is just to . . . give my kids the best chance at success and at seeing the world in the proper way . . . trying to give our kids the best chance

to be successful and have a normal life in terms of treating people the right way, having respect, not getting too bigheaded and feeling like everything's about them."

It would be difficult for anyone even on the outskirts of this bubble to not turn solipsist. And if you're Kevin Durant? One could only imagine. At shootaround the morning of Game 3, he walked off the floor and was heard loudly lamenting to a media member, "If you want fame? Kill KD."

Self-pitying, sure, but not entirely crazy. To quote Joseph Heller, just because you're paranoid doesn't mean they aren't after you. KD had gotten praise for his basketball strategy breakdown and called-shot confidence, but those same forces would feast on his failure. Pride goeth.

Durant would not fail that night, not even close. Instead, he would finish with 38 points, even though he did not play the fourth quarter. This was KD's night of "shots that kill the soul," as Andre Iguodala put it.

After the game, Kerr was asked if KD's outburst resulted from any adjustments made. Kerr said, "Wasn't an adjustment. He had a different mindset tonight than he had the other night. He set a tone right away. Our guys loved it. His teammates were excited about the way he started the game. I think that was infectious, carried over to our defense, too. I thought our defense was fantastic tonight."

Durant refused to relent in the face of a narrative that happened to be true and obvious. When Chris Haynes of Yahoo! asked about how KD had been more of a facilitator of late, Durant interjected, "That's not true." KD's following comment was confusing. "No. I don't pass those shots," he said. "I just play within the offense." His explanation for why he wasn't a distributor in Game 3 was that "coach called more plays for me to start."

"Look, I don't run the show," he continued. "Any team I've ever been a part of, I'm just a player. I'm one of the guys, you know

what I'm saying? Whatever my coach needs me to do, don't matter what it is, I just got to go out there and be prepared for it mentally or physically. Tonight was no different."

This was a master class in Kevin being Kevin. He was publicly undermining his coach, again, but this time by saying his actions were merely the result of whatever his coach wanted. So continued the cold war between Kerr and Kevin. KD was slighting his coach, and his coach had resorted to communicating his game plan wishes through the media. Kerr was happy to keep conveying the preferred shot totals if it would coincide with performances like Game 3. This was dysfunctional but seemed to somehow be functioning. Either Kerr was to be blamed for the poor state of their relationship, or credited with finding a workaround that provoked the desired results. Or Kevin, the open book that nobody could read, was just doing as he pleased, in the moment, for no exact rhyme or reason.

The league was shifting under everyone's feet, and many experienced actors were confused on how to navigate the changing realities. It was an age of "player empowerment," a time when athletes were highly cognizant of their leverage and "platform."

A few prominent players had taken to conducting themselves with increasing outward bitterness. Durant's former teammate Russell Westbrook, famous for his angry playing style, was striking against any questions asked by *The Oklahoman* columnist Berry Tramel. Tramel did not quite know the provenance of this strike and kept asking his questions, getting "next question," in response every time at these press conferences.

The Thunder beat the Blazers in Game 3 of their first-round matchup, saving themselves from an 0–3 hole. As Tramel began his question of Westbrook, Russ, who sat next to Paul George at the podium, ignored Tramel as he conducted a conversation with his teammate. When Tramel finished asking, Westbrook, again,

said, "Next question." Tramel asked again, only this time West-brook scanned the silent room for another question. A Thun-der PR official finally invited one. When the next reporter asked George about his exclamation dunk at the end of the game, he replied, "Next question."

"It's spreading," captioned *The Oklahoman* beat writer Maddie Lee when she tweeted video of the exchange. There were calls for the league to do something about this, but what could it realisti-cally do? Westbrook had shown up to the press conference. He wasn't cursing. His non-answer was technically an answer. He had fulfilled his duties to the letter while spitting on their spirit.

Like my KD controversy, this clip kicked off debates between media people and fans about whether we had a right to answers for our questions. Hiding in plain sight was the deeper dynamic: Players had lost faith in the process. Guys who once were happy to broadcast their fame now felt put-upon by the downsides of the transmission. They were surrounded by people telling them their value and insisting that it could be better optimized. Super-stars were forming their own media companies and talking about becoming owners. What was the media but a nagging, oft pasty middleman, standing between them and the people?

Maybe they were right, but in the meantime, the end prod-uct of these press conferences likely wasn't good for the league. The NBA wanted winsome heroes beamed into televisions across the world. They didn't want sneering, petulant dicks. And, while the league could withstand a few villains, and maybe even benefit from their heel turns, the spread of dickishness was a problem. Insisting that the players were right to act like dicks, or that the media deserved the wrath, did not mitigate the monetary down-sides of dickishness on a big stage. Football had Tom Brady and Russell Wilson "aw shucksing" their way through press confer-ences. The NBA had its biggest stars somehow merging the aloof

with the confrontational. If basketball once seemed like the nation's most accessible sport, something was changing. Walls were coming up.

Ratings fell significantly in the 2018–2019 season, down 26 percent in the first week of the 2019 playoffs. No doubt much of this had to do with the fact that the LeBron James Lakers had missed the postseason. But the mere fact that he'd made the decision to move to Los Angeles—when he could easily have signed with a title contender like Philadelphia or Houston—underscored that there was a different problem lurking inside the league. Winning wasn't enough for James. He wanted to expand his brand, and the public could sense that his journey wasn't about the winning they valued. As superstars were pulling inward, audiences were pulling away.

The Warriors kept winning. But still, the players weren't happy, and the current NBA made that part easy to see.

After the Warriors' Game 4 victory at Staples, I spotted Kerr cleaning junk off the ground in the coaches locker room. All the other coaches had left a trail of half-eaten catered feed boxes and emptied Modelos. "You don't have someone for that?" I, an asshole, teased as the guy was trying to be conscientious. "Hey," he said, with a mock scowl. "How about you get in here and clean this shit up!"

I told Steve that my life was debasing enough as a media member, and then referenced Russell Westbrook's "next question" approach. "I think it's dangerous for the league," Steve responded. He then indicated a willingness to speak publicly about it, giving the following monologue:

"I just feel that we have to be very careful as a league," he said of Westbrook's approach. "We're in a good place right now. Very popular. Fans love the game, the social dynamic, the fashion. But

more than anything they love the connection they feel to the players. I think it's important for the players to understand that it's a key dynamic to this league. I don't think this is a healthy dynamic, for this league, for any player, any team, any local media, any national media.

"It's all part of the business. You've got to feed information to the fans. You don't have to give a great answer, but it's dangerous when you go down that path of no communication because one of the reasons people like the league right now is we have a lot of great players, really good guys who handle themselves well. So don't kill that. You've got to keep that going. That's a big part of the business."

I was curious if this was all different than it had been, back when Kerr played in the 1990s. "There's always been this stuff," he countered. "There's always been players and media members having issues and maybe non-responses, whatever," he said. "I don't think this is brand-new, but we're in an era where there's 24/7 access, and that access is what's driven revenue so much and players need to remember that."

Was Kerr correct? Possibly. Then again, the American public knows comparatively little about football players and it hasn't dampened its hunger for the sport. As *Collision Low Crossers* author Nicholas Dawidoff wrote of the NFL, "There may be no activity that draws closer public scrutiny that the public knows less about."

Many pundits and fans were keen to dismiss the dreary spectacle of regular, compelled NBA press conferences. On Bill Simmons's podcast, Bill would frequently posit that we never get anything interesting out of them. "I'm asking, what are we getting out of any of this stuff?" Simmons said to Ryen Russillo after the Westbrook imbroglio happened. "How many times have you been enlightened or heard anything where you were like, 'Wow. Wow.

That was a moment." He added, "It's so fucking stupid! Why do we do it this way?"

I was sympathetic to that point of view, certainly. I selfishly yearned for the day when we might eliminate these public media availabilities, when so much of my life wasn't squandered waiting for what amounts to a glorified conference call meeting. I could not go so far as to reject their necessity, though.

Sadly, given the soap opera the NBA was selling, these press conferences were probably needed. I couldn't help but notice how often the intriguing press conference bits made their way onto the *Pardon the Interruption* side scroll. Players often took the platform as an opportunity to make grand statements, or, in the case of Kevin Durant, to vent. It was all part of sport's unscripted allure.

Beyond the allure of occasionally good theater, the compelled press conferences likely helped in more subtle ways. Take Klay Thompson, a star with a high approval rating among fans. Klay would never have done a single media appearance if it were up to him. Early in his career, he invariably tried to sneak out of the building after great games. When I asked why he avoided press conferences even after his best nights, Klay looked at his shoes and muttered, "Because I'm not good at them."

Klay slowly emerged from his shell as the Warriors kept winning. He still did not favor doing media, but he was increasingly better at it, if accidentally so. The bits that seeped out of Klay's press conferences helped the sporting public understand a persona. Here was an apathetic, charismatic, half-wise, half-oblivious, Keanu Reeves character with a jump shot. Aspects of his personality that would hardly seem notable, such as his love of Harry Potter, literally the most popular book series of its time, got aggregated as news. His weird malapropisms ("This thing will be in the past like a ponytail") and space-out moments delighted the fans.

Had Klay never been compelled to do media, he would be a blank slate, about as opaque to the public as your standard Pro Bowl offensive linemen. Perhaps he would have preferred it that way, but the league likely wouldn't. In order to connect, Klay had to be pushed.

And so the media merry-go-round continued. Which meant that confrontations over little things happened as often as games. And meanwhile, there was the small matter of actually trying to win.

With the Warriors up 3–1, this series was supposed to be over. Instead, the Warriors shat the bed. The Clippers scored 37 first-quarter points against a listless resistance. Kerr took out a red-hot Kevin Durant late in the third quarter, electing to go with his standard substitution pattern. There were murmurs of disapproval in the crowd. The Warriors, who were surging at that time, faltered down the stretch. Overall, KD finished with an all for naught 45 points. It was an odd quirk of the KD era. When Steph had great games, the Warriors would almost always win. When KD had great games, it really could go either way.

If this Warriors team featured a joyless way of winning, unexpected losses certainly didn't help.

She wasn't wrong. After the game, in what else, another press conference, a reporter from ESPN Brazil asked a question that inspired a quite uncharacteristically haughty reaction from Kerr. When queried about his team's identity, Kerr responded, "What's the identity of our club? Back-to-back champions. We're really good. I mean we're hanging banners. We play fast, we play defense. Maybe we should do an instructional video and send it to you."

The problem with the reporter's question wasn't that it was silly or off base. The problem was that the question cut a little too close.

These home losses to lesser opponents had become part of the Warriors' identity. This was not a team that played with "joy," that feeling Durant mocked in March. This was a team that often just went through the motions, playing at half speed because the game had become a chore and because, well, they could.

Not only had the Warriors taken on an identity of hubristic complacency, but it seemed like Kerr had less and less purchase over whether this could even be corrected. After Game 5, there were locker room grumblings about his choices. The next day at practice, Kerr did his usual media availability, and through the din of some background music over the speakers, he asked of PR head honcho Raymond Ridder, "Hey Raymond, can you turn the music down real quick?" This request sent Ridder scurrying off. "Blue Laces 2" by the recently murdered rapper Nipsey Hussle kept blaring over the speakers, distracting Kerr as he tried to take questions. Unable to hear, Kerr said, "Sorry, hang on," and called Ridder over.

It was explained to Kerr, "Draymond said he wants the music up." Poor Ridder was conflicted, running back and forth between scrum and volume control area, unsure of what to do. Ridder confirmed, "Draymond said he doesn't want it down."

Reporter Janie McCauley jokingly interjected, "Who's in charge here?" Kerr responded, "Clearly not me."

"Enjoy the music," the unhappy coach said caustically, as he walked away.

Practice music had been definitional to the Kerr era. Kerr had introduced it after seeing his friend Pete Carroll run Seahawks practices with high-energy tunes that fueled the vigorous drills. The music, or at least the regularity of its use, was unprecedented in the NBA. Hard-bitten coaches like Tom Thibodeau, who visited preseason Warriors practices in 2015, were shocked

by practice-as-concert. Music was all part of Kerr's Warriors as the happiest of vanguards.

Now, music was being used to mock and undermine his authority. The three championships had not elevated Kerr in the eyes of certain players. One was literally tuning him out.

From the beginning, Steve and Draymond had a fraught dynamic. The most telling microcosm may have happened at the Warriors' first championship parade, when Green was ever sauced and loose. From my (unfortunately titled) ESPN article "Golden State's Draymond Green Problem":

When it's his turn to address the crowd, Green, victory cap slightly askew, shambles across the podium, snatches the mic and declares that he's excited to be speaking. Golden State PR maestro Raymond Ridder, Green explains, "tried not to let me talk today. He know I'm gonna get controversial."

And then he proceeds to validate most all of Ridder's fears: "With these guys, everything's fun. The only time it's not fun is practice . . . film . . . games . . . bus rides. I'm the only person that gets talked about what shots I take and all those things by Steve Kerr. Like, every time I take a shot, he complains. So that's why, if you see, every time I make a shot, I look at him. Dude complain every time I take a shot."

From his seat on the stage behind Green, Kerr shrugs and loudly counters: "Twenty-four percent!" Which just happens to be Green's 3-point shooting percentage during the final three rounds of the playoffs.

Green chuckles, bounds over, grabs Kerr from his chair and drags him to the podium. There are hypothetically a few drops of tension to be wrung from this moment. "This my guy," Draymond starts, prompting Kerr to pat his chest. "From the start of

training camp, he hated me. That's no lie. He probably still hates me. That's no lie. But we going to keep winning these championships—and that's no lie."

Kerr, who's been gamely laughing at the display, steals the mic. "You know how they start to play music at the Oscars when it starts to go on a little long and security comes and grabs the guy? That may happen here in a few minutes. Thanks, though, Draymond," he finally offers, before fleeing for the safety of his seat.

That relationship wasn't helped by Green having the best run of his career in Kerr's absence, when Luke Walton took over the reins as Kerr recovered from a spinal surgery gone wrong. Walton let Draymond shoot sans critique, and Draymond shot it better. Kerr, who'd rather Green move the ball, came back and criticized shot selection. The two would nearly come to blows on February 27, 2016, at halftime in Oklahoma City. "I am not a robot!" Green yelled at Kerr. When Kerr told him to sit down, Green screamed, "Motherfucker, come sit me down!" He went after Kerr, and teammates separated the two. Among other niceties, Green yelled, "Suck my fucking dick!" at his coach.

The two moved on from their fraught past and won a couple of championships, but 2018–2019 was a less happy team than past iterations. Earning double-digit millions does not protect the middle-aged man from such indignities. He had to wear these slights because he needed Draymond. Did Draymond still need him?

In the end, whether it was Draymond or KD, the practical result was worth the trouble. KD finally closed the series with a staggering 50-point barrage over and through everything the Clippers tried against him. As Kerr, a former Michael Jordan teammate, put it after the game, "That was one of the great performances I've ever seen in my life. And I've seen some good ones. I've been around some decent players."

After the game, you could have expected some modicum of happiness from the victorious superstar. He was finally getting those "best player in the world" accolades, even from his own coach, who had long since stopped worrying about how such praise reflected on Steph's reputation.

Still, KD was smoldering, still angry at my boss Tim Kawakami and yours truly for who knows what and ranting about it to colleagues. After the game, Anthony Slater, another colleague, interviewed Durant, who was, again, obsessed with media coverage.

"Everything we do is high-profile," Durant said. "And I don't believe anything was ever wrong with our locker room. No offense to you two guys, but every time your [media] colleagues walk in here, they bring that toxic energy in here and they start writing about that energy because it's how they feel.

"But when you're actually in this locker room, there's nothing going on in here. We just be chilling. There's a lot of speculation about me, about my attitude, about where I'm playing next season that a lot of these dudes in here [points around at random media members] are trying to distract us with and then want to blame it on me because it's easy to blame it on me. I understand that. We understand that. So for us, we just made it about basketball."

Fair enough, but there was always a contradiction here that few ever called him on, in person at least. He just wanted to focus on basketball, but kept ranting to media about media critiques. He didn't care about what was written, but would endlessly discuss its toxic impact. His take on Patrick Beverley's defense was similarly confusing. It wasn't that Beverley was in his head; it was that people saying Beverley was in his head got in his head. From the interview:

"It was just the, 'Oh, don't let him get in your head,'" Durant said. "That's the thing with me now, the criticism of me now. Because people can't really criticize the basketball. So the criticism is that he was getting in my head."

He then makes an admission, laughing a little while doing so because he knows it sounds a little contradictory.

"So, you know, I actually was getting into my head because of people saying that," he said. "You know? Stop talking to me about somebody getting in my head because it didn't happen."

Wherever the outside rhetoric drove Durant's brain, the result has worked perfectly for the Warriors. He entered Game 3 with ferocious intentions, hitting five jumpers in the opening minutes—"Kill mode," Draymond Green called it—and he kept that same energy for four straight games.

Did he come out with a point to prove? And, if so, does he feel like it was proven?

"Uhh, I don't really have those thoughts when I come into this game," Durant said. "If you haven't watched me in 12 years, I feel sorry for you. Because you've missed some good performances over this time. I don't have to prove nothing. If I don't play well one night, just come back the next."

Durant's spiel wasn't all that logical, but he had attained a level of on-court greatness that compelled illogic's indulgence. We all had to pretend, to a certain extent. This was the Kevin Durant experience. It wouldn't have been such a strange road for the organization and surrounding media if he was worse. But he was great, mostly as an individualist. In theory, an abundance of ego undermines team goals. In reality, the team was thriving as Durant's ego raged on. As KD said in the Slater interview: "People don't like how I am, don't like how I approach shit. Don't like how I don't smile. How I just don't have this exuberant spirit, how I

don't make them feel good about coming to a game. But that ain't my job. My job is to be locked in on me, be focused on me."

It was hard to disagree with such a historically awesome individual player. In this situation, he really only needed to be focused on himself. He certainly had that part covered.

Durant and the Warriors' success did cast some doubts on the value on the entire enterprise, the joy that preceded the task in general. If winning just comes down to talent and if the reward is misery, then what's the point? Is the point just money? Fame? To what end?

If anyone within the Warriors cared about these questions, they kept that hidden. In the end, what keeps one sane is focusing on the task at hand. After the game, I ran into Bogut in the hall. He was also talking about Tim Kawakami, this time from a positive perspective. Tim, though politically liberal, had bucked against some reflexive fan criticism of the San Francisco 49ers' drafting star defensive end Nick Bosa. Bosa had right-wing tweets in his past, more than a few of which he deleted in anticipation of joining a Bay Area team. Bosa had also ripped celebrated black artistry like Beyoncé's music and *The Black Panther* movie. Perhaps these were fair opinions in isolation, but given the context of other tweets, they were bundled into an argument that Bosa was of a certain nefarious perspective. Was Bosa racist or unfairly maligned? Kawakami offered a realist perspective in an article:

> I do not think social media activity from three or four years ago, assuming that Bosa did not outright state racist or homophobic thoughts himself, is an NFL disqualifier. I believe the 49ers locker room can and will accept him if he accepts the culture of the 49ers' locker room.
>
> Also, if Bosa is a great player, much of the locker room and the fan base will be quite ready to embrace him, anyway. That's

how football works—you want to play with the guys who help
the team win.

In the end, athletic might makes right. What's good for the team
is what matters. The part Kawakami didn't mention, but anyone
who'd been around football could tell you: most white NFL players
shared Bosa's political leanings. "There are more Republicans than
you'd think," Bogut said with a wink, when I brought this up.

The same rules applied, whether it was Nick Bosa or Kevin
Durant. Nearly everything was subservient to in-game production. That was the beauty of sport and also the downside. The
path to a title can be littered with little moral and emotional com-
promises. The Warriors, its fans, and surrounding media would
pretend some wonderful things about Kevin Durant's personality
and general outlook, so long as he produced and remained in
blue and gold. The 49ers, its fans, and surrounding media would
set politics aside so long as Bosa reliably gave quarterbacks crip-
pling injuries. This was a brutal world and all that mattered was
whether your guy could devastate the other guys. Perhaps Kevin
Durant was most correct when he sarcastically interrogated
Kerr's "play with joy" ethos. There was no joy in the world, only
winning. KD did not make sense sometimes, but he often had
a point.

Earlier in the series, Durant had said of his matchup against
Patrick Beverley, "With this series, it's kind of weird because when
a guy's that small, you've got the advantage, but the referees see
David and Goliath. We hear that story a lot growing up, so that
story is prominent in people's minds. When you put that out on
the court, the ref's going to give him a little bit more. So, when he
runs up on me, grabs me, holds me, I don't mind it. That's how he
makes his money. That's how he feeds his family. But if I throw
something back, then let us play. You know what I'm saying?"

He had a point there as well. It reminded of Wilt Chamberlain's "Everybody pulls for David. Nobody roots for Goliath" lament. Maybe nobody roots for Goliath, but when he wins, they can hardly deny him. The David loses more often than not and gets forgotten. Nobody will be telling their grandkids about Patrick Beverley's efforts in a series. The sands of time would blow over his efforts soon enough. Kevin Durant's legacy would linger longer. The Clippers were history, and the Rockets were next.

The Rockets pissed the Warriors off. This was a mistake. Heading into the Western Conference Semifinals, Houston had a shot. They were the less talented roster, but had pushed a more unified Warriors team before. Not only that, but the Warriors had worn on the refs very thoroughly over the season. Perhaps that could be dismissed as irrelevant to a team's chances, but the Warriors had truly taken their ref scorn to another level.

On a near nightly basis, Draymond and KD went at refs like they were the opponent. The team's March 29 loss in Minnesota featured a moment where Steph Curry made a game-tying three, which he celebrated by pointing and laughing at the refs for having denied Durant a call on the play before. Curry called ref Mark Kogut "the MVP" in his postgame comments. Durant referred to ref Leon Wood as "the best player on the floor" in his postgame comments, adding "Great call Leon" on an Instagram video of his foul.

This was a different level of aired ref grievance, somewhat indicative of the team's competitive arrogance. Other teams might not feel so entitled to a certain level of treatment from officials. Other teams might worry about angering the insular, tight-knit Philly-based reffing community. If the refs were important enough to be bitched at, they were important enough to sway outcomes. Yet the Warriors carried on as though they alone controlled their future destiny.

The refs were to feature prominently in the Warriors-Rockets series. Many of James Harden's lurches into defenders are subjective scenarios. Could be a foul by the letter, could be a non-call by the spirit. What the ref decides can determine whether the Rockets offense succeeds. Could the fraternal order's loathing of the Warriors turn a series?

The Rockets did not waste much time squandering whatever goodwill they had with the refs. After the Rockets' Game 1 loss, Harden said of the reffing, "I mean, I just want a fair chance, man. Call the game how it's supposed to be called, and that's it. And I'll live with the results."

After the Harden press conference concluded, my colleague Sam Amick wrote an article titled "Sources: Rockets' Game 1 Ref Rage Rooted in Extensive Warriors Research." Specifically, the Rockets were furious about Warriors defenders getting into James Harden's "landing area" on three-point attempts. Amick's article details how the Rockets compiled an extensive memo after they lost Game 7 of the Western Conference Finals in the last postseason.

From Amick's article:

When that series ended nearly a year ago, the Rockets' research had just begun. They secured the play-by-play officiating reports from each game from the NBA—a service that is afforded to individual teams (teams aren't given reports for other teams, which makes it hard to compare). These reports document the league's verdict on correct calls and missed calls in the same way as the Last Two Minute reports that are shared publicly, with the obvious difference being that it accounts for all 48 minutes of action.

And after the Rockets went through every line, tallying all the missed calls for each team and adding up the potential points

that were lost along the way, it wasn't pretty: The Rockets, according to the sources, had a double-digit point deficit in six of the seven games (and a small edge in Game 2). In all, sources say, they were harmed to the tune of 93 points. Game 7 was the worst, the research showed, with the league-issued report indicating they should have had 18 more points. More specifically, two of the 27 consecutive missed 3-pointers that did them in were ruled to have been missed foul calls.

The point totals were deduced by the Rockets after their own research based on data given by the league.

Even Warriors haters ripped the Rockets over this complaining. It is difficult to gain righteous sympathy in defeat, but especially over a game in which your team famously missed twenty-seven consecutive three-pointers. Not only was the memo whiny, but also earnestly ridiculous. It faulted the refs for not calling a foul on the Rockets because, in the ensuing possession, the Warriors made a three-pointer, which is worth more than two free throws. The memo also fit the stereotype all too perfectly. To certain observers, here was Daryl Morey, king of analytics, attempting to claim the intellectual vanguard of whining. It looked like a man trying to mask his basic bitching as some law of physics, an attempt to reframe subjectivity as an objectivity that magically favors your team.

On ESPN's *High Noon*, cohost Bomani Jones said of Morey, "He's acting like a dork." Jones added, "Nobody else is writing book reports. Only Daryl Morey is out here trying to crank out some regressions in order to try to make this happen. Because the goal of this is to get something in your favor. You've got to take the pulse of the room and in this room, the room's the world. You have to be able to realize, 'Dude, I'm about to look like a big old dork right now.'"

Perhaps Morey would have caught less flack if James Harden wasn't already regarded as Morey's system-gaming basketball avatar. Harden was already known for flopping on drives, but this controversy shined a light on how Harden also tends to launch himself forward on jump shots, an obvious foul-seeking manipulation. Harden might see it differently. In his interpretation, the rules are the rules, and there is no spirit to be violated. From a February 2015 Lee Jenkins *Sports Illustrated* feature titled "James Harden, the NBA's Unlikely MVP":

> "Oklahoma City taught us to chin the ball, so when you lay it up, no one can strip it," Harden recalls. "I did that for a while, but it didn't work for me, so I started putting the ball out instead. People kept reaching for it and hitting my arm. It was like finding treasure, finding gold. Everyone thinks I'm looking for contact, but I'm not. It's bait on a hook. You have the option to reach for the ball. But if you get my arm, it's a foul."

Behind the scenes, Bob Myers fixated on how the Rockets were circumventing league rules by pushing their complaints via the media. Couldn't everyone see how the Rockets were sneakily breaking the rules? The answer was that nobody really cares about that part. For a former agent and a smart individual, Myers could be a bit of a true believer, mystified by the state of how things are. He wasn't one to cultivate media relationships in the way other GMs did. When stories like this emerged, he was often confused as to why the narrative was what it was.

Whether the Rockets circumvented league rules did not matter. What mattered was that the public considered the Rockets morally wrong because they appeared weak and dorky. The Rockets, in between *Dungeons & Dragons* dice rolls, were invoking a hypothetical scoreboard, about as offensive an act in the eyes of

fans as any. That they were violating the spirit of arcane league rules to do it? Not such an offense.

Before Game 4, Warriors Ops men gathered at a table for a pregame media meal, the cafeteria-style grub teams offer to those with press credentials. Rockets owner Tilman Fertitta is a restaurateur, and he ensures that the media spread at the Toyota Center is among the best. It's one of the rare arenas that does media food of a high enough caliber that Ops men might partake. The near entire Warriors FO was something to see. They were all nattily attired, sitting upright. With their tailored suits and styled hair, Bob Myers, Larry Harris, Mike Dunleavy, Kirk Lacob, Jonnie West, and Nick U'Ren were out of place among the frumpy media set. They were apart, in a *Mad Men* scene of their own, absent any smoking. Adding to the *Mad Men* effect, every table sitter was white, male, and looked like a plausible former Prom King. These were life's winners, vested with the responsibility of picking the sport's winners.

If you're around the game, you know of the racial split between Ops and roster, one very white, the other quite black. The reasons for the demography can be debated, but the reality of it can't be. That's not to say Ops is exclusively white and male; it's just especially so, in a way that could be less noticeable in another field. The split might have louder critics if the power dynamics were clearer. As in, if Ops had clear authority over roster, the racial split might be more bemoaned by pundits. In this modern era, it was difficult to answer the question of whether that table or the locker room had more power. The locker room certainly earned more money, with Steph Curry alone claiming a $201 million contract. The locker room had more control of the future, with Durant putting these table suits on tilt at his whim, year after year. In the NBA, nobody was more powerful than a superstar, certainly not GMs and not even your average owner.

In contrast, the other, more replaceable players were beholden to the whims of the Ops men. The suits had to continually assess and analyze these players as though they were widgets, trading and cutting them according to whatever marginal advantage might arise. The term "assets" came into NBA world vogue around Sam Hinkie's reign in Philadelphia. In media, players were increasingly discussed in the language of financial markets.

Naturally, some players started to resent this trend, combined with the racial dynamics involved, with a few ascribing it all to the "analytics" movement that had gotten so popular. In a *New Yorker* interview with Isaac Chotiner, former player and current ESPN TV analyst Jalen Rose said of the analytics movement,

> There are many people that feel like it has a cultural overtone to it that basically suggests that, even though I may not have played and you did, I am smarter than you, and I know some things that you don't know, and the numbers support me, not you. Two, you notice that, when it is a powerful job in sports—whether it is an owner, whether it is a president, whether it is a general manager, whether it is a coach—usually in football and basketball, sports that are primarily dominated by black Americans, it's also an opportunity to funnel jobs to people by saying that, "I am smarter than you because the numbers back up what I say, and I am more read. I study more. I am able to take these numbers and manipulate my point."

Rose also made his case for why a playing career could give great insight into other jobs within an organization, saying, "There is no bigger experience than being in the foxhole, in the huddles, and out on the floor—being a part of the game plan and being game-planned against."

Rose might have been correct about this and other points, but it wasn't clear if his assessment applied to the NBA level. Of the final eight teams in the 2019 playoffs, none had general managers who had played in the NBA, though a few were formerly high-level players. In their Ops hiring, the Warriors did not prioritize NBA experience, though Mike Dunleavy Jr. had played for the team. It just wasn't something that mattered to them nor probably, increasingly, to other franchises. The same might be said for "diversity" in general, though many involved in the league paid public lip service to the concept. The catechisms of the modern public square were often at odds with private practices.

The Warriors Ops men were all facing the same direction, watching the Boston Celtics lose Game 4 to go down 3–1 to the Milwaukee Bucks, effectively ending the Celtics' season. ESPN's Brian Windhorst strolled past the Warriors table and quipped, "Kyrie Irving's free agency begins today!"

That got a blast of hearty laughter out of the men of Warriors Ops. At the same time, there was likely some chagrin at that table. The Warriors had affection for the Celtics, perhaps more so than any other team. Celtics general manager Danny Ainge had helped Myers get the Warriors job, Joe Lacob had been a minority Celtics owner. In preseason I'd asked FO members who the best coach was. The most common answer was Celtics coach Brad Stevens.

Yet, for all the belief in the Celtics, they were going down in flames. On the way out of the media dining area, Myers asked me what I thought of the series. I simply said that the Bucks were just a lot better. Not exactly trenchant analysis, but Giannis Antetokounmpo plus supplementary talent looked a hell of a lot more formidable than the scrappy Celts plus a depressed Kyrie Irving. Bob grimaced. The Celtics were done, but the Warriors, in many ways their progeny, were still very much alive.

And yet Kyrie's dissatisfaction with the Celtics situation had implications for the Warriors. Durant and Irving had been linked as a pair, a package deal. If Irving was on his way out, KD would almost certainly follow.

The Houston home games were slogs, detested on an aesthetic level by Kerr. The use of isolation basketball offended the coach's sensibilities, though he felt it was needed to counter the Rockets' switching. The tactics took a toll on the Warriors' offense, which appeared more stagnant and less potent.

That wasn't all the Rockets were successful in doing. Durant is a brilliant player, good at everything save for seeking hard contact. So the Rockets sought out contact. Stout mini-big P.J. Tucker continually crashed the offensive glass, sneaking behind KD to extend possessions and exact punishment. The Warriors appeared to have no answer for this problem.

Game 4 was another loss for the Warriors. Down three, in the waning seconds of that one, Curry drove in and took off for a badly missed dunk that would be mocked the world over. Curry looked diminished after Durant started asserting himself.

The whining about the refs had come and gone. The series was back on.

Nobody quite knew whether the 2018–2019 Warriors would fail. If it did happen, though, nobody could say there was an absence of signs. In many ways, the demise seemed foretold. We had already seen the divisions, and the lack of satisfaction fueling the effort. The playoffs were supposed to cure all this.

With the series tied 2–2, with the Rockets having won the last two games, the Warriors appeared to be orchestrating yet another disappointment at home. After rushing out to a 20-point lead, they slowly gave it all back. Again, Curry looked uncomfortable and struggled to hit shots. Again, Durant was getting boxed out of the

picture on rebounds. At the 2:12 mark in the third quarter, KD hit an isolation jumper over Iman Shumpert, a mundane, predictable outcome considering the size difference. What happened next terrified Warriors fans, as Durant whipped around and looked back at his right leg in a manner common to Achilles tears. He would exit the game, and begin life as a mysterious *Waiting for Godot*–type figure, out with a lingering "calf strain."

In the meantime, the Warriors had a game to win. Suddenly, they had verve down the stretch as Steph Curry surged back to life. The Warriors weren't a "better" team without Kevin Durant, but they did regain some purpose. The Game 5 victory saw more of a collective, frenzied late-game effort than outings in the past.

Afterward, rumors persisted that Durant had indeed actually torn his Achilles. Basketball Ops guys from multiple teams called me to make inquiries. They were suspicious of the diagnosis. One went so far as to tell me that his team had kept watching the play on repeat, blown up in slow motion, to isolate what looked like an Achilles tear.

I found their suspicion suspect. For one, Durant had left the building that night quite calmly, even if he eschewed doing media. From everything I knew about the man, a season-ending injury would not have been taken with equanimity. Also, he had left under his own power.

The Warriors were doubted going into Game 6, with Vegas making them 7-point underdogs. The prevailing conventional wisdom was that absent KD, the Dubs might be done for. Instead, they ended Houston's season, with Steph, Klay, and the bench coming up huge. Klay hit the game-sealing shot and bounced around, pointing at Joe Lacob in his baseline seat. Joe pointed back. Moments later, Curry also pointed at Lacob, only Lacob did not see the superstar because he was turned around, busy

high-fiving Warriors officials. That was more or less the dynamic for years. Lacob, by accident or intention, extended more love to the first draft pick of his ownership reign than to the better player who preceded his presence.

Joe Lacob turned toward me outside the locker room. "They say we don't have a bench," he said, pointing. "That. Is. Bullshit! You can quote me!" The Ops men had wanted Kerr to give some of the bench players more run during the season, but Kerr was reluctant to trust. It had not been a major rift, but perhaps a subtle tension. Durant's absence finally compelled the use of a larger rotation, and it worked under pressure. "I probably should have used them earlier," Kerr said of his reserves after the game. Kerr, not feeling much regret or tension, would call this his favorite game he ever coached.

It was only a second-round clincher, but the team's celebration was otherwise something bordering on orgasmic. The locker room was a wild scene. When I asked Klay why the celebration was so revved up, he, as he often did, gave the most succinctly correct answer: "Because that shit was *hard*." As Dr. Alan Grant once said in *Jurassic Park*, "T. rex doesn't want to be fed. He wants to *hunt*." For some time, the Warriors had craved challenges beyond their own boredom. Durant's absence had made the game harder, but also easier to get up for. Not only that, but the KD circumstance finally lowered expectations. The doubted are praised effusively in victory. The believed are merely acknowledged when they win.

Audiences thrilled to the KD-less game, which rated as ESPN's most-viewed Semifinals telecast ever. Many pundits and fans made the same point: the Warriors were not improved for lacking Kevin Durant, but they were certainly more fun to watch. To paraphrase John Lennon, nobody was saying the Warriors were "better" without KD, but maybe, just maybe, they were bigger.

People had missed the old Warriors, a team with chemistry and vulnerability. The pre-KD Warriors were a fantastic team whose

whole was greater than the sum of its parts. The Kevin Durant Warriors were an unbeatable team whose whole was not greater than the sum of its parts. Nonpartisan audiences may have preferred the former.

The good times kept rolling in the next series, with the Warriors overwhelming the depleted Blazers. On Fox Sports, Chris Broussard said of the Warriors success, "Kevin Durant's worst nightmare is coming true." Durant tweeted in response to Broussard, "I see a little exaggeration there buddy, my worst nightmare?? U sure that this is the worst that it can get???" What followed was a bizarre public debate between the two over whether Broussard's direct message conversations counted as texting conversations.

While some rushed to KD's defense, I couldn't help but be amused by the initial phraseology from Durant. He wasn't even denying that it was a nightmare, just that other hypothetical nightmares were worse. Also, everyone deep down knew Broussard was correct, whether they wanted to cop to it or not. A Warriors championship without KD would be disastrous to Durant's reputation. It would put the entire KD-era run in a less flattering light. Was that fair? Probably not, but that's how sports talk works.

KD was simmering in absentia, feuding in direct messages with a colleague over the question of his importance to the team. You could understand his frustration. Not only could he not do what he loved, but outside forces were indeed incentivizing him to root against his own team's success. Most in his situation would be rooting against their teammates. Athletes at this level don't want just to win. They want to be the reason for winning.

The Western Conference Finals against the Blazers appeared to confirm this narrative: the Warriors dispatched the overmatched Trail Blazers in four games, all without Durant. By the end of the series, Kerr was playing eleven guys, again successfully drawing off that Strength in Numbers gestalt.

When the sweep was achieved in Portland, Kerr, still abuzz over the Houston series, told me, "I love how that series ended. Game 6 was one of my favorite games that I'd ever coached. Because, Kevin isn't there and our bench comes up huge."

Kerr then made an aesthetic distinction between playing the Rockets with Durant versus playing the Blazers without him. "I didn't enjoy the Houston series, but I also felt like it was necessary to play that way to beat Houston," he said. "I hated playing everybody forty-plus minutes and not trusting the bench, but I think Houston forced us to do it."

I could barely hear Kerr's comments, as they came amid a noisy crowd near the Moda Center loading dock. Many Warriors family members and friends were in attendance. The closer a team gets to the ultimate goal, the more the postgame milieu swells. Kevin Durant was not there, but damn near everyone else with any connection to the Warriors was.

Even in these moments, both the Warriors and the media knew that Durant was important to the team, and talk of a championship without him always felt unrealistic. Realism was about to arrive in the form of a team far better than the Blazers.

In the Finals, against the Raptors, the Warriors faced an opponent complete enough to punish their weaknesses. Signing Durant had meant sacrificing much of the depth that preceded him. Even if Joe Lacob believed in the Warriors bench, there was only so much it could produce after Klay Thompson missed Game 4 with a hamstring injury. The Warriors would fall down 3–1 amid many whispers about why Durant was still missing from the fray.

Durant's teammates were mostly confused about his health status because he'd so cut himself off. They did not know much more than the public about an athlete who appeared outwardly quite healthy. The "Where is KD?" whispers grew louder after it

was announced that Kevon Looney, thought to be done for the series with fractured cartilage in his collarbone, was actually returning to the NBA Finals. Klay Thompson's insistence on playing through a hamstring strain added to that narrative.

Kevin Durant would finally make his return to the Finals. As he entered Toronto's Scotiabank Arena for Game 5, it felt like a scene from a royal wedding. Media onlookers lined his path from the loading dock area, flashing cameras and recording the walk-up of a stoic man on a mission. It was a hero's entrance, the making of a modern-day Willis Reed.

With Durant back on the roster, the Warriors could start Draymond at center, something they had been avoiding all series due to their lack of size elsewhere on the roster. The Warriors are really only *the Warriors* when Draymond is pushing the ball from the center spot. KD might have cut himself off from the team, but his return allowed it to recapture an old cohesion.

Durant hit two three-pointers with ease, part of an initial run where the Warriors canned five consecutive triples. Their early offense was smooth and forceful. In that first quarter, the improbable comeback from down 3–1 did not look so improbable. It might have even seemed like a fait accompli. It certainly felt that way to the Raptors fans sitting near me, who lamented how they would now lose the series with typical Canadian sports fan self-loathing. The Raptors were probably better than the Durant-less Warriors. With KD in the mix, not so much.

All was well until Durant made a move on Serge Ibaka and his right Achilles exploded. The crowd roared as KD lost the ball and tumbled to the ground. Many of the home fans kept cheering the injury as Raptors players attempted to scold their own crowd into better behavior. KD would stoically limp to the locker room, joined by Curry, Iguodala, and a very haunted Director of Sports Medicine Dr. Rick Celebrini. The Warriors would go on

to win, in thrilling late-comeback fashion, but it was a Pyrrhic sort of victory.

Bob Myers wasn't exactly celebrating the W when, after the game, he conducted a tearful press conference. "He was cleared to play tonight," Myers said of the disastrous outcome. "That was a collaborative decision. I don't believe there's anybody to blame, but I understand this world. If you have to, you can blame me. I run our Basketball Operations department."

Myers likely felt badly for not just Durant, but also Celebrini, who was well regarded within the organization, and under fire for what happened. The shaken doctor had cried in the locker room. Of Durant, Myers continued, "The people that questioned whether he wanted to get back and play were wrong. He's one of the most misunderstood people. He's a good teammate and I'm lucky to know him."

When asked of Durant's emotions, Myers said, "Sports is people. I know Kevin takes a lot of hits sometimes, but he just wants to play basketball and right now he can't."

Even in this insane, tragic scenario, the meta conversation about KD was inescapable. "Fuck them. Fuck them," DeMarcus Cousins said when asked about the "people" who questioned Durant's heart during the time he missed. There was a certain externalization of the blame, as though nobody within the Warriors was asking the kinds of questions many fans were. Warriors players did not know what to make of Kevin Durant's injury status because they did not know what to make of Kevin Durant. In the end, he really was compromised and being held out for good reason. It was a hell of a way for everybody to find that out.

At the same time, media was perhaps partially to blame for what happened, but not because there was an abundance of criticism, or "hits" as Myers might put it. Indeed, it was the opposite.

We had all collectively set a praise trap. We were the ones who lined the locker room path, creating a cinematic entrance for a resurrected hero. We turned a return into a surreal myth-making opportunity. You sensed it in the hush that fell over the gawking media, followed by the murmurs when Durant appeared. It was the perfect soundtrack for Durant looking like a boxer in his dark hoodie, head tilted downward as he made his epic trot as the TV cameraman followed.

This would be hard to resist for most people. You go from spectator to heroic protagonist just like that. We would not join forces in assailing Durant's character for missing the Finals, had he sat out. No, that's too taboo a thing nowadays in this more sensitive media epoch. But we would sure as shit praise the guy to high heavens for returning, especially if he won. That was the carrot we, the media, the fans, and also his peers, all dangled. It turned out to be poisoned.

In an Instagram post, Durant would comment on his situation and the night's victory, saying, "I'm hurting deep in the soul right now I can't lie but seeing my brothers get this win was like taking a shot of tequila, i got new life." It was an endearing message from a guy who'd given his all. Warriors fans loved it. The many who had expressed annoyance at his mood swings and tendency to quiet Curry's influence on the action had come away from the disaster with a renewed respect and appreciation.

This was the night of Kevin Durant's redemption and also the consummation of his Faustian bargain. For years, he'd wanted love and recognition from a fan base that wanted Steph to be the hero. On June 10, 2019, Kevin Durant was finally *their* hero. It just so happened to cost him his Achilles tendon.

The Warriors would be eliminated in their next game, a game where Klay Thompson suffered a comparable disaster, tearing

his ACL off a third-quarter dunk attempt. Klay had hit two free throws with his knee shredded up and tried to stay in the action. This further burnished Klay's legend as a myopic badass.

When the Raptors sprung their "Box and 1" defense that prioritized Steph and little else, the remaining players couldn't produce. The dynasty, at least the version that had the league demoralized, was over. After the game, Joe Lacob walked into the locker room for an aside with Curry, whose late missed three-pointer sealed defeat. Lacob wrapped his arm around Curry, and complimented Steph for how hard he fought and assuring him that what happened wasn't his fault. It was the rare, visible moment of tenderness in an otherwise outwardly cold relationship.

Later, in Lacob's Bridge Club room, Warriors VIPs attempted to have something resembling a cathartic party, the last one ever, with Kerr and family drinking and reminiscing. The official word on Klay's ACL tear flashed across the TV screen in the room, drawing boos from the Warriors VIPs. This wasn't just a loss. It was a horror show. Careers were in jeopardy. The opening season at Chase Center was shot. A dynasty that was in the process of dying a natural death had expired quite violently. It had gone little by little, then all at once, leading to an anguished howl instead of a last hurrah. On June 13, 2019, the Warriors left Oakland for good. On that night, it seemed like they'd left a lot more than a city behind.

The Warriors would have to move on from what they once were. The question was whether they would do so with a radical restructuring or instead as a diminished version of their glorious past. The combination of Kevin Durant leaving and Klay Thompson getting hurt forced their hand. Big moves were necessary and imminent. The dynasty was over, but life had to continue. It was Bob Myers's job to build a new civilization out of Rome's rubble.

7

THE KING OF "I DON'T KNOW"

THE WARRIORS WON SO MUCH WHILE HELMED BY A GM WHO proclaimed to know so little. Perhaps that isn't a coincidence, nor is it a coincidence that such winning happened absent that general manager making such success a story about himself. When it all finally collapsed, the franchise would rely on the guy who sublimated his ego to go and make some ballsy moves. Uncertain times called for a man whose expertise was forged in uncertainty.

After the NBA Draft on June 20, 2019, media and fans were treated to a Bob Myers press conference that contained more shrugging indifference than reassurance. Of the team's three selections Myers said, "If one of them gives good minutes, great. If two can, great. I don't know. Who knows who that guy will be? But we like these three well enough, and if they can help us next year, great. If they can't, hopefully they'll help us the year after." Fans and attending media were a bit confused. These press conferences are typically optimistic, happy occasions. Myers, perhaps distracted by the massive machinations involved in Durant's imminent exit, wasn't bothering to show much faith.

Around the Warriors, it was an open secret that Bob Myers had been operating in a state of exasperation. He had done so well in his role but success offered little relief, and perhaps diminishing rewards. "It's a monster job," Myers told me during the 2018 NBA Finals, which his team was easily winning. "Even when you succeed, it's daunting. It's hard. You look around, anybody that takes this job in any professional sport. There's an enormity to it, that lasts. Our mistakes live on for years." He wore that pressure. Those close to him spoke of it, but even if they didn't you could see it on his face.

Being a general manager isn't what you think it is. It's not at all like playing fantasy sports, an ersatz version of a GM's job that many fans find exciting, gratifying, and even sustaining to their friendships. In theory, it's a decent enough facsimile. You're drafting players. You're making trades. For a certain type of American male, this seems like an ideal life. You make millions of dollars and operate as the technical boss of world famous athletes, and have action on every game. What could be better?

It just so happens that almost no one is actually happy doing it.

"I fucking hated that job," Steve Kerr said of his reign as Phoenix Suns GM. "So much stress, so much drama. The day I quit was one of the best days of my life. I drove home that day, Phoenix to San Diego, in ecstasy." Kerr then pantomimed lifting his arms in the air as he rocked out to Counting Crows.

Kerr didn't just quit. He fled the state. He found far more fulfillment in being a head coach, a famously stressful occupation.

"It's all great sitting in your office, but what happens when your two stars are at each other's throats?" says Blazers GM Neil Olshey. "Can you walk down to the locker room and mediate that? When your owner is at his wit's end with your coach. Can you talk both of them off the ledge, right? That's the art of this job. The art of this job is to be really good at it, you have to be able to deal with

everyone. You've got the people that work in your practice facility, and you've got your scouts, and then you've got the media, and then you've got your doctors, and then you've got . . . you're managing your owners, or multiple owners. And then, you've got to go down, and deal with a player. Then, you got to deal with their agent. You've got to be a chameleon."

The simplest summary of why being a GM sucks is that it's all encompassing. Manage up to your owner, and down to your coach. But it doesn't just stop there. The organization has dozens of employees you're theoretically responsible for.

You'd better check in on them and make sure they're all pulling in the same direction. Meanwhile you should probably watch a shitload of basketball. You'll need to know what you're talking about in those meetings. And by all means, get your ass out on the road and start scouting college prospects. The owner is going to ask you about them come draft time and you'd better have some good responses. Speaking of the draft, it can happen roughly a week after the NBA Finals concludes and roughly a week before free agency starts. You must always operate on multiple timelines. Try not to descend into madness as you focus on your team's current season simultaneously with your team's future plans. Just know that if you win the championship, your coaches and players will party in Vegas while you attend NBA Draft workouts. Oh, and could you please make the minority owners feel included? Sure they aren't the main honchos, but they're paying a lot of money to be part of this. It's time for your conference call. Meanwhile, you'd better talk to the media. Something bad and public just happened within your organization and it's time to get out ahead of it. The fans need to feel secure in the team's direction. Just don't divulge too much of your future plans because you can ruin your leverage or get fined for free agent tampering. Does the Fantasy NBA team seem preferable yet?

On June 18, 2017, Draymond Green paced about the victory parade stage, a place where he's known to go stream of consciousness on the state of the Warriors. Wearing a shirt that read "Quickie," a reference to his team's decisive five-game demolition of the Cleveland Cavaliers, Green scanned the small crowd of Warriors officials, seated on the stage. Without segue, he said, "Can somebody give [Warriors GM] Bob [Myers] some fucking credit?" The crowd roared, titillated by the surprise profanity at a family event.

In using the word "credit," a buoyant, sloshed Draymond mentioned something Myers tries to eschew. Myers, a former UCLA bench player, is fond of John Wooden's quote, "It is amazing how much can be accomplished if no one cares who gets the credit." He will reference it often when asked questions about how this team is able to accomplish so much. In an ideal world, credit eventually flows to those who reject it.

Does that happen in reality? Did credit ever arrive at Bob's doorstep on a level commensurate with his accomplishments? It's a hard thing to measure, but probably not. He's well liked. High approval rating with Warriors fans, certainly. Widely respected around the league. But, there's a reason why Draymond felt he was not being fully appreciated.

Bob built his career a few hundred feet from Oakland A's executive Billy Beane's Coliseum office, but is still not as famous as Billy Beane. In his first seven seasons, Bob boasts seven playoff berths, five Finals runs, and three championships. Beane, the protagonist of Michael Lewis's best-selling *Moneyball*, has no championships, but was played by Brad Pitt in a movie. Lewis's writing talent has a lot to do with this reputational chasm. Many sports executives would cite how Beane branded himself, claiming that the real market inefficiency Beane plumbed was self-promotion. There's also the matter of narrative, how the Oakland A's are, by

dint of their own frugality, underdogs. Beane might be Sisyphus, perpetually toting depleted means to no ultimate end, but he's made that plight look like KD's favorite parable, David versus Goliath. It's a neat trick by Beane, one that apparently only requires that David fight valiantly. Myers might have presided over a miracle turnaround in Oakland, but few see it as a long-odds triumph.

One of Myers's few failures is in the arena of GM branding. He doesn't have a *thing*, a calling card general managers usually need to enter the public consciousness. In the NBA, GMs are usually background, unless they were once foreground. Jerry West is widely celebrated as perhaps the greatest general manager of all time, but his fame is augmented by having once been a superstar player. The Celtics' Danny Ainge is known as a man who'd trade anyone away. This is a contemptible trait in some spheres, but a quality fans can love, with some showing Ainge the very allegiance he witholds from players. It's also a brand that was likely only made possible by his previous experience on the 1980s Boston Celtics. (When talking about potential deals and draft picks, Ainge often draws on comparisons to his playing days alongside Larry Bird and Kevin McHale.) Nobody cares if some pencil pusher GM shows little loyalty to players. A former player? That's juicy!

The Heat's Pat Riley is nicknamed "the Godfather," and, with his hair slicked back, very much looks the part of a charismatic mafia don. His winning reputation was forged as a successful coach for the 1980s Showtime Lakers. Pat Riley wasn't just a winner. He was *cool*, wearing Armani suits in an era when most coaches dressed like absent-minded professors. Not only did Riley's coaching success augment his GM "brand," but that brand did considerable work for him. Riley famously threw his championship rings on the table when he successfully pitched LeBron James on joining the Heat.

Raptors general manager Masai Ujiri has a *thing*. Perhaps he hasn't quite penetrated the American sports consciousness, but he has defined a persona to NBA fans and it's an enviable one. He's the closest thing to a James Bond figure at the NBA's executive level. The Nigerian master trader has a biography unlike anyone else in sports. He strolls into a Finals game with Barack Obama, who rumor has it wants Ujiri in DC so the two can join forces. Masai is sharp, Masai is slick, Masai is often referred to by his first name alone, because that's just the kind of cachet Masai has. Is he famous yet? Maybe not, but he's been ready all his life for the role. Fame and acclaim suit Ujiri, and he's earned it by now.

If you don't have a *thing*, you'd better have a concept worth selling. The influential corporate set enjoys reading about sports management. *Moneyball* made for the frequent flyer's perfect airplane tome. Unlike the other jobs in sports, management is one these white-collar types could envision themselves doing. It's also the one they could see themselves learning from and applying to their own PowerPoint presentations. *Moneyball* taught corporate warriors across the world how to look for a market inefficiency, the ultimate romantic quest for a certain kind of person.

For a general manager to transcend his sport, he needs an interesting, publicly known idea. A general manager isn't a player and he isn't a coach. To the public, he's an idea man. So what's Bob Myers's big idea? Nothing quite sticks the way it does for some other modern GMs.

Nobody at the business college teaches a class on Bob Myers's vision of Warriorball. If there *is* a trendy NBA GM strategy that aspiring corporate chieftains thrill to, it's probably "The Process," former Sixers general manager Sam Hinkie's paradoxical ouvre. Hinkie subverted the league by having his Sixers lose big in pursuit of high draft selections. He amassed "assets" in novel ways,

leveraging a longer timetable than other teams dared. In the end, Hinkie ran out of time. He was forced out, right before his talent-laden roster took off. After resigning from his role with the Sixers, Hinkie went on to teach a business class on negotiations at Stanford.

While Sam Hinkie never won a championship and was ultimately removed from the team he built, he lives on as a celebrated sports martyr. Local fans turned him into a cult hero—the man too smart for the NBA world. His likeness appears on hipster T-shirts, and his nom de guerre, The Process, is arguably Philadelphia's biggest basketball star, even bigger than its best players (though Joel Embiid, also nicknamed "The Process," is close).

I know Sam a bit and I suspect part of him will be forever sick over how it ended in Philadelphia. Reputationally, though, he's in the catbird seat. It's obvious to fans that his crazy plan brought talent to a barren roster. Any failures from here on out will be attributed to the regime that took over. Not only did Sam Hinkie game the system, his legacy did as well.

Hinkie is the protégé of Rockets GM Daryl Morey, who happens to be the NBA's answer to Billy Beane. Dubbed "Dork Elvis" by Bill Simmons, Morey was an instant star executive, a leader in the field almost from Day 1 on the job. As with Beane, *Moneyball* author Michael Lewis has a little something to do with Morey's uncommon renown among GMs. In a much talked-about February 2009 *New York Times* article titled "The No-Stats All-Star," Lewis profiled the secret, nuanced impact that role player Shane Battier provided on Morey's Houston Rockets. The article was less a profile of Battier and more one of a general manager whose elevation represented a sea change in sport. Leslie Alexander, owner of the Rockets at the time, had been a market-inefficiency-exploiting Wall Street investor. His hire of Morey was an orthogonal assault on the ways of the league. From the article:

"We now have all this data," Alexander told me. "And we have computers that can analyze that data. And I wanted to use that data in a progressive way. When I hired Daryl, it was because I wanted somebody that was doing more than just looking at players in the normal way. I mean, I'm not even sure we're playing the game the right way."

Daryl Morey wasn't just hired to win. He was hired to pioneer. In that, he succeeded. Morey's teams did much to pull the greater NBA away from midrange jumpers and toward more efficient options like three-pointers and free throws. "It's changed the game, right?" Michael Lewis said on Simmons's podcast of Morey's measures. "The game is played differently partly because of Daryl. Just the realization of the efficiency of the three-point shot has opened things up."

"Moreyball" doesn't quite have the subversive cachet that "The Process" does, but Morey's extreme emphasis on three-pointers and free throws helps differentiate him from the other GMs. While Morey has not won a championship, the Rockets are reliably good. Unlike Hinkie, Morey's squad never "tanked" in pursuit of a rebuild, so not only is Morey a gate crasher, but he's a dependable fan pleaser.

Key to his legend is Morey's founding of the Sloan Conference, an annual celebration of analytics at the MIT business school. The event has grown from a small, self-consciously nerdy jobs fair to the kind of shindig Obama gives speeches at. Morey is now bigger than basketball. He didn't just shake up the league as a nerdy outsider; he created a movement. Every year, young, aspiring quants pour into Sloan, with designs on running the lives of athletes they couldn't possibly relate to.

On Sloan's website, a passage of its founder's biography reads, "Morey revitalized the Rockets in 2012 by acquiring James Harden

via trade from Oklahoma City. A total of 17 transactions were required to set up the trade with the Thunder, including the creation of the league's first reverse protected draft pick (guarantee to land in the lottery)."

Not only does this passage flaunt the success of Morey's homerun Harden trade, a decision that bet on Harden's statistical profile over the conventional wisdom that believed he was coming off the bench in Oklahoma City for a reason, but it boasts a different kind of triumph. Morey is lauded here, not just for his vision, but also for his complexity. He is commended not just for his coup, but for his arcane "reverse protected draft pick" innovation. A "reverse protected draft pick" sounds more likely to cause the next financial crisis than net you an MVP, and that's sort of the idea. The young (mostly) men of the Sloan Conference are inspired by the concept of high-level arbitrage. It's like being on the vanguard of the financial services industry, but way cooler.

The Sloan types became the league's Young Turks, bitterly resented by the jockocracy of former players who had been running things prior. For decades, jock executives could claim a certain authority over their nerdy tycoon bosses. The analytics revolution quickly eroded jock authority, mocking their traditional ways as stupid and anachronistic. The jocks couldn't quite hold back the nerds, who keep joining organizations at lower levels and moving up. The jocks might have had height, fame, and testosterone on their side, but the nerds can actually speak the language of new money owners. If your boss made his way in private equity, you're better off talking assets than assists.

Which brings us back to Bob Myers, a classic basketball man. There's no concept attached to Bob, at least not a popularly known one. There's no tale of arbitrage. In a counterintuitive way, his self-presentation almost cuts against the formation of legend—not because he's slovenly or ugly, but the opposite. "He's a handsome

fucker," Daryl Morey told me of his competitor. "He makes us all look bad."

Myers just looks like one of life's winners—nattily attired and well coifed. If a GM looks like a man for whom life comes easily, it's not such an easy parable to sell. If being successful is just simply something you are versus something you can learn, the Sloan Conference might as well close up shop.

To say Myers lacks a concept attached to his name does not mean he's without guiding principles. He is fueled by certain ideas, notions that inform his reign. It just so happens to be someone else's ethos. Myers has a Gregg Popovich quote from 2014 saved on his phone:

> A synergy has to form between the owner, whoever his president is, whoever the GM is, whoever the coach is. There's got to be a synergy where there's a trust. There are no walls. There is no territory. Everything is discussed. Everything is fair game. Criticism is welcome, and when you have that, then you have a hell of an organization. That free flow through all those people is what really makes it work. And that includes everything from draft to Os and Xs. Nothing should be left to one area—only to the president, only to the GM, only to the coach—or the culture just doesn't form. At least that's what's worked for us.

Bob Myers believes in this stuff. It's all too subjective for the Sloan set, to be sure. Trust? How do you quantify trust?

When asked about the quote, Bob says, "Of course, the Spurs are a paradigm. They're so fascinating, because I think they've done a wonderful job of winning, but at the same time, just of enjoying this lengthy journey of twenty years." When asked about whether some observers might scoff at the use of "trust" in a hard-bitten competitive business, Myers responded, "If people want to think

it's corny, that's fine. The alternative would be a mercenary type approach, and I'm not sure how well that lasts in any organization. I think it's a short-sighted way."

Myers has tried to implement such a culture of trust. It's why he's visible everywhere in the organization, smoothing over every rough edge he can find. It's why he'll ask the young analytics staffer to send him ideas on improving the team. Everyone has a purpose and can contribute some value. Myers has no grand, overarching concept, apart from traditional ideas of people building off one another, in concert. Beyond that, he has the will and personality to actually manifest the virtues of such clichés. When egos undermined basketball utopia, it was Myers who solemnly took it upon himself to hold it all together. It was Myers trucking off to a road game in Utah when Draymond and KD were at loggerheads, attempting to broker a lasting peace between fraying factions. In these moments, Bob made his impact less as an idea man than as a perpetual merchant of maintenance.

I remember seeing Myers at a preseason game shortly after he took over the team. He was wearing a sleek suit and gabbing into an earpiece a few seats in front of me. I figured he was some kind of slick confidence man, which isn't exactly a novel persona in the NBA. From a distance, I could see him schmoozing with players and other NBA personalities. He ended every interaction the same way: a hand would clasp over his interlocutor's shoulder, and Myers would tilt his head back in laughter at some inside joke. Then he'd stroll over to the next person of importance and greet him heartily, starting the process anew. On the surface, the new Warriors GM looks like a cool agent archetype.

Then you talk to Bob and the voice doesn't quite fit the look. It cracks a bit and is absent much projection. If you speak with Bob, the most common phrase you'll hear is, "I don't know." In one fifty-minute interview for this book, he used it a dozen

times. An example: "I don't have the hacks for being a GM. I don't know what I'm doing. I just try to do it the way that feels the best for me. Maybe it's completely wrong. I don't know. Maybe I should change it all. I would not stand up amongst my brethren and say, 'Do it like this.' Maybe I should do it like they do it. I don't know."

If Bob tells you something, it's often "for the sake of edification." Bob is often seeking his own edification. He tends to ask questions, almost out of nowhere. He wants to know what you think of the team, and where they might be vulnerable. It's not a challenge, though I'd often felt put on the spot. He's legitimately curious. Maybe you'll hit upon something that nobody else has noticed.

Words like "edification" aren't commonly heard in the NBA jock world. In doing business, you're advised to forget the poly-syllabic terms. Sage Warriors assistant coach Ron Adams, a man of extreme erudition, once complimented Andre Iguodala on having a "rapier wit." In what would become an oft referenced running joke, goofy backup center JaVale McGee incredulously responded, "He has a 'rape her' wit!?" It's not that most people in the NBA are stupid; there are many savvy operators. It's just an environment where so much study is confined to the court.

I've seen Bob operate in different spheres and he does so with ease. Nothing changes, yet he somehow fits anywhere. Coaching mega-agent Warren LeGarie, whom Myers worked with in a prior job as an agent, says, "He doesn't change because he's not duplic-itous. You know how some agents and GMs, all of a sudden they get around black guys and they get into the vernacular? One of the things he learned, when we used to be in the offices at SFX, and Rob Pelinka would be on the phone going, 'Yo wassup, dawg! How you be, man?!' We'd go, 'Isn't there a middle-class white guy here? Where'd he go?' But with Bob, I've never met anybody more comfortable in his own skin."

Pelinka, GM of the Lakers, has turned into something of a bizarro Bob Myers. At the event level of NBA arenas, you often hear Bob contrasted with his evil twin Rob. Articles compared the two when Pelinka was hired by Magic Johnson in March 2017. Like Bob, Rob worked as a young gun for superagent Arn Tellem. Like Bob, he left the agent world to run a West Coast NBA team. Pelinka has the well-put-together look down too, drawing appearance comparisons to Rob Lowe.

It didn't go quite as smoothly for Pelinka in LA, for reasons that might be partially attributable to the differences between the two men. Myers is fairly genuine and Pelinka is something less than that. There was much eye rolling around the association when Pelinka started quoting high-level books in his press conferences, mostly because it was done in a manner that looked more like affectation than communication. "I've had many conversations with Rob," said one GM, laughing. "Books never came up." In one example that certainly had Warriors officials cackling, Pelinka, at the press conference introduction of role player shooting guard Kentavious Caldwell-Pope, described his latest signee in the following way:

> I would venture to guess there's people in the room that are familiar with the stories in the Book of Genesis, where there was a time when the Israelites were wandering in the desert and all of a sudden, bread came down from heaven. That's kind of what today feels like for us to have KCP join.

What Pelinka didn't mention was Caldwell-Pope's affiliation with free agent target LeBron James. KCP was a client of Klutch Sports, the agency started by James and childhood friend Rich Paul. Few regarded Caldwell-Pope's one-year, $18 million contract as some bargain for the Lakers, unless "bargain" meant price

paid to secure LeBron James's superstar services. The move read as LeBron placation, not some savvy standalone signing. For whatever reason, though, Pelinka had to lay it on thick, presenting an intensely cynical process as miracle manifest. Also, the book was actually Exodus, not Genesis.

Myers doesn't behave this way—he shies from the spotlight rather than seizing it. And perhaps an examination of KCP's season illustrates why.

That season, Caldwell-Pope would plead guilty to violating the probation he'd incurred from an earlier DUI conviction. For a brief stretch, Caldwell-Pope was taking part in a work-release program as a means of serving his twenty-five-day sentence, and not allowed to leave the state. That may have been an embarrassing situation for the Lakers organization, but well worth it, in the end. LeBron James would join the Lakers that summer. KCP would sign another one-year deal, this time for $12 million.

It's difficult to divine exactly why Pelinka's artless bullshit was received so poorly by the league. The NBA's executive level is replete with colorful characters, and many a wheeler-dealer type. It's hard to have a real conversation with a GM or coach without hearing "He's so full of shit" about somebody else. If this is a league of frauds, then what's one more?

It wasn't even that Pelinka had been a bad agent. Many thought he'd been a fine agent, highly aware of his clients' needs versus market realities. There was just something incongruous and unconvincing about Pelinka's brand of agent-GM, something about agent sleaze combined with GM's responsibilities that put people off.

On January 28, 2019, superstar Anthony Davis, another Klutch client, informed the New Orleans Pelicans that he would sign with another team when his contract came up in summer of 2020. In the meantime, he was requesting a trade. From a distance, this was a novel exploitation of leverage for Pelinka, Paul, and Davis.

Teams would be wary of trading pieces for Davis unless they explicitly knew he'd re-sign. This meant that the Lakers could rig the game in their favor. If Davis would sign with nobody else, then they were the only team capable of confidently exchanging real value for him.

That's a fine gambit for an agent. If the plan follows script, the hardball tactic is rewarded and the client gets what he wants. If the team refuses? Well, in the NBA, teams usually cave to superstars, even while getting dumped. There's no point in holding on to a player who wants out, especially when you depend on his agent for other deals. From the agent's perspective, all that matters is giving the client his desired outcome. And in this case, the Lakers and Davis had exactly the same goal in mind. What could be more perfect?

What followed was a protracted humiliation for the Lakers, LeBron, and the league. It turns out that teams react a bit differently when an opponent attempts a hostile takeover of their roster. After some consideration of Lakers trade packages, the Pelicans refused to play ball. Salary rules dictated that Davis could only sign with the Lakers in 2020 at a highly reduced rate. So the Pelicans called his bluff. There were enough other teams desperate for Davis that they'd trade good value absent a guarantee to re-sign. The trade deadline passed and no deal got done.

By the middle of the 2018–2019 season, the Lakers were imploding. Reports indicated that team morale was crushed after it was learned that most of the roster was offered in an unconsummated trade. Sure, players are dangled in trades all the time, but this one was different. LeBron was perceived as a partner in Klutch operations and influential in the Lakers' strategizing. To these mostly young Lakers, it wasn't just some upstairs suit who'd attempted to upend their lives; it was their most important teammate.

This isn't the kind of issue an agent worries about. LeBron (client) and Anthony Davis (client) had their objectives. What could the downside be in trying to pursue those objectives? The issue is, of course, that a team is about more than the wants and whims of its best individuals.

Pelinka's narrow focus would eventually get its big win, but at a cost. The Pelicans' firing of Dell Demps, combined with the hiring of David Griffin as GM, opened up communication between the Lakers and Pelicans. Two days after the NBA Finals finished, a deal was done. Anthony Davis would be a Laker, and three young Lakers (Lonzo Ball, Brandon Ingram, and Josh Hart) would be shipped off to New Orleans. Their feelings were a matter for New Orleans to concern themselves with. All the draft picks the Lakers added to make it happen? A matter for future people to concern themselves with. Pelinka and LeBron won the here and now. During the Anthony Davis saga, Bob Myers had been linked to the Lakers as a possible replacement for Pelinka, but the Lakers stood committed to his evil twin. Maybe they were right to, in the end. Maybe Myers wouldn't have been the right former agent to successfully navigate a dysfunctional organization.

When asked what's different about being an agent versus being a GM, Olshey, a close Myers confidant, immediately gave a speech on the matter, hardly pausing to breathe:

Well, I think when you're dealing as an agent, you may have a client roster with twelve or fifteen guys on it. But one player couldn't give a shit about the other player, like this player's in a silo. Like, if Bob Myers represented Jermaine O'Neal, Tracy McGrady, and Brandon Roy. He never dealt with them as a collective. So, whenever he dealt with each of those guys, they were the center of the universe. But if you have Kevin, Draymond, and Klay, and Steph, you have to know that when you're talking to one of them, it's

within the context of the collective. And you can't be seen as playing favorites. When you're an agent, you're basically playing a favorite every single time you get on the phone with Bryant, as far as they're concerned. Right? You are the most important person, the most important client. Your family is at the forefront. Your deal, your marketing deal, your contract is all they're thinking about while you're communicating with them. Then, you hang up the phone, and you move on to the next guy, and you make him feel like that. But if you try to do that in the NBA, constantly trying to micromanage each individual player in a vacuum, without it being within the context of the team, and the organization, then you look like a sycophant, right? One who's running around playing favorites. Because, you're not going to treat them all equitably, because they don't all deserve equitable treatment, within the context of the team. Because, not all players are created equally, in terms of their impact in the organization. So, you have to make, like Quinn Cook feel as good as you do with Steph. But you're not going to give them the same accommodations. But as an agent, if you had Quinn Cook, you would expect to be treated no differently, or he would go find another agent.

This sort of balancing act was a real challenge for GMs, the kind of thing Fantasy Players need never worry about. Over the summer of 2018, the Houston Rockets lost Trevor Ariza, a theoretically key role player, to free agency. Though not a star, he was a 3-and-D guy, an important commodity for any contender. There were multiple reasons for why this happened, but it's worth noting that Ariza was frustrated with what he perceived as unequal treatment.

As Zach Lowe said on his ESPN podcast on May 25, 2018, "I did this big profile on Trevor Ariza in the playoffs. And this didn't make the story, but a lot of people told me that Trevor Ariza is like

a basketball purist. He was compared frequently by members of the Rockets to a Gasol brother. So I asked, what does that mean? And they said, one of the things that irritates Trevor in Houston and elsewhere, is that we're all going out to dinner, and even though it's a team and it's a family, there are different rules for superstars than there are for everybody else. Superstars get stuff that we don't get. And he's just sort of had to swallow his idyllic vision of what a basketball team should be, even though that kind of stuff [annoys] him."

Smoothing out such tensions is where Myers excels, but how does an organization measure that? How does a GM get tangible credit for working out issues too delicate to be broached in public?

"You have to be Henry Kissinger to be a general manager," Olshey says. "That's where the art of this comes in. It's not only putting it together, but then having the ability to manage it, on a macro level. And how do you mediate all this stuff? Because, you can't be seen as, 'Well, he's always defending the coach.' Or, 'He's always defending the players.' Or, 'He's doing the ownership's bidding.' You always have to be seen as, 'I see what he did here, and deep down, I know it was for the good of the team, and the organization.'"

Olshey and Myers talk regularly, despite running opposing teams in the same conference. Olshey worked his way up from workout guy to GM, and has seen much of the league from inside out on that journey. The two hail from a secret NBA fraternity, a circle within the circle: self-made GMs. These are the men who lacked a birthright to basketball, in their estimation.

"As much as Bob is at the top of the mountain now, he still has the persona, right, and all the core values of a guy who had to earn where he is today," Olshey says of his friend. "And I think because he had to earn it, he appreciates it more for what it is intrinsically, without having to go out there, and get the validation publicly,

the way that so many other guys crave it, right? They need that validation from outside sources. Because Bob has kind of become a self-made success story, he doesn't need validation from anyone else, because he's earned it. The guys that need the validation from everyone else are the guys that are silver spoon guys who had standards too."

The "self-made" basketball executives comprise a smaller group than you might assume. The NBA is rife with nepotism and fame-based hiring practices. Owners are impressed by former stars, as are fans. They feel warm and fuzzy about Larry Bird, Magic Johnson, or Isaiah Thomas running their teams. Well, at the beginning they do. It seldom ends well.

But at least it starts. Many a former bench player laments their lack of opportunity. If only they'd played or were somebody's son. If a non-birthright GM finally makes it to the big show, he carries that shoulder chip along for the ride. So, Bob Myers might look like Mr. Easy Street, but because of this path, he has a different self-conception. "My whole life," Myers said in an *LA Times* article on his career, "I've always had to outwork people to be successful."

You might see a six foot eight man who grew up comfortably in the horse ownership capital of Danville, California. You might correctly assume that playing for UCLA opened up some doors for him. From this perspective, Bob is the ultimate overdog. Not necessarily. Myers came to UCLA as a walk-on in 1992 and, over a collegiate career, ground out a path to part-time starter. In between all the hard work necessary to elevate his prosaic skill set to an elite performance level, Myers got to be part of a championship team and have multiple informative lunches with the legendary John Wooden. It was an idyllic run for a walk-on, but for one big issue: it had to end.

Bob knew he loved hoops and didn't want a desk job. He was unclear on the other deals and was looking for a mentor to sort

them out. Enter Arn Tellem, the Los Angeles–based superagent whom HBO's *Arli$$* was based off.

"Coach Jim Harrick, who I was friends with, coached at UCLA at the time," Tellem recalls. "He called me and said, 'I have someone terrific I want to recommend.' I thought he was talking about a player. When he said, 'Have I got the guy for you,' having represented Reggie Miller, I thought maybe I was getting another Reggie Miller. I said, 'Who is it?' Harrick said, 'Bob Myers.' I said, 'Who's that?' Harrick said, 'He's on the team. He wants to be an intern.' My heart sort of sank."

An inauspicious beginning for Myers's postgrad career, but at least Tellem agreed to meet the kid. "When you meet Bob, you're immediately taken by just what a really good, nice guy he is. I gave him the internship and he stayed with me twenty years. We've had an extraordinary run together." For years, Myers did whatever Tellem asked, including getting a law degree from nearby Loyola Marymount. Bob rose within Tellem's empire, emerging as one of the NBA's premier agents.

For all the success, the job never quite matched Bob's personality. He was a natural introvert in a career that demanded absurd levels of extroversion. Beyond that, the job necessitated a certain level of self-promotion that never jibed with Myers's nature.

"It didn't ever feel that authentic to me," Myers told me. "I tried. I think I did it the best way I could, but I never felt like I was great at it or had the necessary skills to sell myself appropriately."

Myers had achieved the dream, just not quite at his dream job. His career, forged by two decades of quite intentional hard work, was a bit of an accident.

"I didn't really want to be an agent," Myers admitted. "I just didn't have any other path to basketball. I suppose I could have coached, but nothing came up. I don't know. It was probably unintentional. I just wanted to be around basketball and I wasn't good

enough to play, and that door opened and I figured I'd walk into it and see where it went. I think it was thirteen or fourteen years."

When Danny Ainge recommended Myers as an out-of-the-box GM choice to Joe Lacob, Myers jumped at the chance.

"Well, we had dinner at Toscana and that's where he broke the news," Tellem remembers. "He told me during dinner. I was sad for me and happy for him. That's how it was. He was the person I was grooming to take over basketball. It was bittersweet. We continued to do well at the agency, but I lost someone who I was very close to and you know for me, some of the enjoyment that I had. Part of the enjoyment is really working with the people that you like so much. That obviously, you know, was hard for me."

Myers was supposed to carry on the Tellem empire. Instead he took off for a position in a famously defunct franchise. Shortly after his protégé left, Tellem would leave his agent business for a vice chairman position with the Detroit Pistons.

There has been a lot of speculation around the league as to whether Bob Myers might have a similar Toscana date with Joe Lacob in the future. Such rumblings quieted after Myers signed an extension with the Warriors in 2019. Before that, he was paid considerably less than Steve Kerr, though neither salary was public. His assistant GM Kirk Lacob happens to be the owner's son, something many GMs might view as working under a Sword of Damocles. There's also the matter of working for Joe, who demands much from those beneath him and has a hyperfocus on the future.

At the press conference for the signing of DeMarcus Cousins, Myers showed irritation when asked about Cousins's status as a "one-year rental." "I know everyone's job now more than ever is to speculate," Myers said. "Our job is to win a championship in 2018–19. That's hard enough as it is. So thinking about beyond— we didn't get these championships by thinking about the next one

and the next one. They are very hard to do. I don't even like the word 'rental' or 'one-year' or this guy's a free agent, that guy's a free agent. Every day, he is on our team. Everyone else is on our team. We're trying to sign one more guy and then win a championship this year. That's it. What happens after that, who knows."

Myers could only handle so much talk of the future when the present demanded so much. Those who know Myers relay that he's less buoyant than in years' past. Winning achieved a great dream, but its fruits did not sustain the soul. For one, a GM is not permitted to sleep, let alone slip off into dream world. The job demands hypervigilance, a perpetual state that more reliably chases away happiness than it does threats to a franchise. The threats will come. Something is always going wrong on a basketball team. It is the GM's duty to put out every fire until one day, his job cannot survive the latest conflagration. It's a thankless gig that also happens to be the biggest one in Basketball Ops.

In Myers's case, while the responsibility was heavy, his powers were lesser than in other organizations. Certain general managers, far less accomplished, were permitted to hire armies of assistants and associates. Bob had to run everything through Joe, and there were no rubber stamps.

Kerr had more power to hire consiglieres and underlings. That's not unique to him. Coaches, even if they are lower on the org chart than GMs, tend to have staffing power. Maybe it's because the coach always knows what he wants, or at least seems to. Chaos favors someone with a plan and sports is filled with destabilized moments. Coaches, for all their neuroticism, generally have tendencies if not outright agendas. An advance scout once said to me, as he chuckled about Kerr's love of the "Weak Roll" play, "Lemme tell you something. Nobody, and I mean nobody, is a creature of habit like NBA coaches are."

In contrast, the NBA general manager has to wing it, maintain a plan on different axes of time, present and future, as the latter is often thrown into terrifying variance by the ever-shifting former. On June 30, 2019, the Warriors were in such a moment. What would come next?

A GM once asked me, "If we agree that a bad coach can win a championship with a great roster, but nobody thinks a great coach can win it with a terrible roster, then why does the coach make more than the GM?" After a pause, I replied, "I don't know."

Yet, someone had to organize the chaos of summer 2019.

8

MAXIMUM CHAOS

For a half decade, the Warriors were all-powerful. In the end, they were passive observers to their dynasty's dissolution as KD made the final call. No matter their successes, they could not ensure health and happiness for the capricious god in their midst. They were not alone in such a plight.

Benjamin Franklin once said, when weighing in on a dispute, "Those who would give up essential liberty to purchase a little temporary safety deserve neither liberty nor safety." The quote often gets cited by those defending privacy from government surveillance, but that fight has little to do with the quote's provenance.

Franklin was warning the Pennsylvania General Assembly against giving up their authority to tax the wealthy Penn family, in exchange for short-term defense funds. The quote has echoed far beyond that local dispute, perhaps because it gets at a counterintuitive truth: there's a massive risk in trading away your own autonomy, even if the purpose is to mitigate risks.

Starting in the 1990s, NBA owners wanted safety, mostly protection from their tendency to sign players to onerous contracts. In pursuing it, they traded away their power. Now, they've never been less in control.

In late June 2019, the Warriors were one of many teams left vulnerable to the whims of a max-level player. In the case of at least four teams, Kawhi Leonard was presiding over their hypothetical plans. In the case of the Warriors, it was still Kevin Durant, as it had been since his arrival.

As Durant's decision loomed, there remained an odd split within the Warriors ranks. Those staffers who traveled with the team had long consigned themselves to the inevitability of Durant leaving. Players would freely say as much in off the record conversations. Coaches were similarly convinced. The most optimism you might hear was the theory that he's unpredictable, so who the hell knows, really?

Even if KD's mind could be changed, among players and coaches, there wasn't a whole lot of motivation to woo him back to the Bay. Joe Lacob, on the other hand, still believed in belief. He wasn't ready to give up. Publicly, he expressed optimism on re-signing KD. Those around him on the higher-level Ops side weren't willing to give up, either.

For everyone else, the focus was more on keeping KD happy in the short term, for the sake of winning a title that season. Few will ever admit to being motivated by factors beyond winning, but at a certain point, winning with misery just isn't an appealing path. Eventually, losing more minus the misery seems acceptable, at the very least.

The KD arrangement had served its purpose, but the story had run out. The Kevin Durant saga was something those "on the plane" Warriors could grin and bear in pursuit of a 2019 championship.

It was not a situation for which there was tremendous enthusiasm behind continuing in perpetuity.

Joe Lacob did not have to live in that world, nor did the other Ops men. So long as Kevin Durant was on the roster, they were in the game. Quickly, they had to pivot when undeniable reality finally reared its head.

Back in 1997, a twenty-one-year-old Kevin Garnett signed with the Minnesota Timberwolves for six years, $126 million. In retrospect, this was good value for one of the greatest power forwards ever. At that point however, the price tag seemed exorbitant for such a young player who still had so much to prove. The other owners blanched and the painful 1998–1999 lockout followed. When it resolved, the "maximum contract" was born.

The "max" contract dictated a ceiling on how much a team can pay an individual player, represented as a percentage of the salary cap. It doesn't matter if LeBron James might have garnered $100 million per year on the open market in his last Cavs seasons. He had to content himself with a third of that.

The owners negotiated for the "max," along with shorter guaranteed contracts in subsequent collective bargaining agreements. For years, there was a trope of owners attempting to "protect themselves from themselves." There had been bad, lengthy contracts handed out. Sports pundits delighted in mocking these terrible decisions. These billionaires just couldn't help but make poor choices, it was reasoned by many observers. Without proper controls, they would get in a bidding war for these elite players, give away the store, and depress their fan bases for long periods of time.

Bill Simmons penned a November 14, 2011, *Grantland* column on the then ongoing NBA lockout. In a section titled "Issue No. 3: Guaranteed Contracts Are Too Long," Simmons wrote,

Even the Players Association seems to agree on this one. Long-
term deals allow players to coast for years on end (how's it going,
Rashard Lewis?), mail in entire seasons (what's happening, Char-
lie Villanueva?), or eat themselves out of the league (would you
like another slice, Eddy Curry?). Any of those paths make the
players look terrible as a whole. From the league's perspective, you
can't have five- or six-year deals AND a salary cap, not when the
wrong contract can singlehandedly submarine a team. Players also
play their greedy butts off during contract years . . . so by having
more contract years and fewer Long-Term Deals Gone Wrong,
the league's quality of play would improve. At least that's the hope.

Simmons wasn't entirely wrong. The long contracts for mid-
dling players of lesser motivation were indeed a bad look for the
league. Before the lockout started, Simmons was downright psychic when he predicted the following, while citing the contempo-
raneous Hollywood writer's strike:

> And sure, like with the Hollywood strike, an NBA lockout will
> end up working in favor of the owners. It will lower operating
> costs, protect teams from overspending and create a system in
> which A-listers get rewarded (the LeBrons and Wades) and the
> working class (the Goodens and Farmars) gets screwed. Costs
> will drop, franchise values will increase, and the owners will
> believe all the acrimony was worth it. The ship will have been
> righted. Or so they will say. I hope they're right. I still don't know
> how it benefits you and me.

The 2011 NBA lockout did end up working out for the owners.
Franchise valuations skyrocketed from that point forward, with the
Los Angeles Clippers selling under duress for $2 billion in 2014, an
unthinkable sum just a few years prior. The A-List players indeed

reaped bigger rewards, though they would see the largest gains would perhaps come under the Chris Paul–led union in 2016.

Thanks to restrictions on contract length, owners would no longer be saddled with commitments that weighed their teams down for more than half a decade. There were risks to signing certain players of course, but the pain was over more quickly, and more tolerable. As Simmons theorized, the players might have performed better too, considering how there was always another contract around the corner.

And yet, there was a catch to all of this.

Risk and reward are often correlative in life. NBA superstars, blocked from attaining long-term security, started to dabble in the wonders of the shorter-term commitment. The issue for owners, the issue that never really goes away, was the unassailability of superstar value. No matter what structure owners attempted to impose on the NBA superstar, that superstar still had a massive influence on wins, far beyond what other stars in other sports could boast. This ability will represent itself as leverage, no matter what. The superstar had something the owner wanted, really something the owner *needed* if they were at all interested in winning championships.

"Life finds a way," as *Jurassic Park*'s Dr. Ian Malcolm said, and the same is true for value. Worth will express itself, roughly in proper proportion, regardless of rules meant to contain it. A super-star potentially adds hundreds of millions in revenue to a team, to say nothing of boosted social relevance. Joe Lacob was able to privately finance an arena in the last good piece of land in San Francisco because of Steph Curry. Dan Gilbert was able to build a casino in downtown Cleveland because of LeBron James. Both men got to brag about winning a championship, which they might describe as "priceless."

When LeBron James left Miami to rejoin Gilbert's Cavs, he did something unprecedented. James, in a clever bit of salary cap

manipulation, elected to sign deals one year at a time. From a July 21, 2016, *Cleveland Plain Dealer* article by Joe Vardon on James's pioneering of one-year deals: "The stated intention at the time was money—James wanted to put himself in position to earn the most financially in every season and capitalize on the coming explosion in the salary cap. But James also extracted for himself a certain amount of leverage in Cleveland, holding over the front office the threat, however remote, that he could leave the organization if he felt there was not a commitment to winning."

The one-year deal was a game changer, an apotheosis of long-term trends. By leaving Cleveland the first time, LeBron demonstrated a willingness to hurt local feelings in pursuit of happiness. The backlash was incredible but James ultimately survived, as did his reputation. The move gave LeBron leverage. Who could now doubt his willingness to leave at the drop of a hat? It also gave leverage to other superstars. A precedent had been set, which fueled a kind of social contagion among elite players.

Unusually candid NBA veteran Jared Dudley told me over the phone, "I'm not surprised players almost want shorter contracts now. And because of that, players have more power. Players are flexing it. We're doing that and it's now gotten to a point where someone like Kawhi [can] change the game, say hey, I'm only playing sixty-five games and he's telling you *before*. He's *telling* you how he's going to play. I love it to a certain degree. Owners are making money, players are making money. I think that, you know, the old generation probably doesn't like it because there's no team."

Superstars were indeed starting to see themselves more as atomized "brands," for whom sports teams were mere vessels. Rising sneaker contracts were a factor here. Not only was the sneaker business based on selling a player's individuality, as opposed to his ability to bond with teammates, but it made an athlete less reliant on team compensation. If superstars were capable of earning more

money from Nike than, say, the Cavs, that reduced the motivation to lock into the slightly bigger contracts a player gets from re-signing with the team that drafted him.

Finally, the one-year deal was the move of a highly prized mercenary, someone who might rather command than commit. It made sense that Kevin Durant opted for one-year deals in Golden State after LeBron James started the trend. Steph might be the man in Golden State, but KD could have all the power. The "contract year" had traditionally been viewed as a player-motivating time. In truth, the contract year cut both ways. Teams were likely to lay on the incentives and charm in that final season of a superstar's deal. With one-year deals, players could get that treatment in perpetuity. Is the coach really going to dress you down in front of everyone when you might leave? Why not have that arrangement every season? Why not use it to get your friends hired within the organization? Why not have anyone and everyone in your friend group on the team plane? Under the one-year deal, lines of ownership blur. The player of a certain caliber has ultimate authority. He took on the risk of the one-year deal. Your perpetual fealty is his reward.

And really, why wouldn't the players act this way? The owners weren't paying them out of the kindness of their hearts, even if they tried to talk in terms of "family," "loyalty," and "love." In this world, the emotion is quantifiable, represented by cash. I once saw an owner take a player aside after he had a big game. I asked the player what the owner said. "He said he love me." I asked how the player felt about that. "I don't trust that motherfucker. I'll see how much he *love* me this summer!"

The Warriors had loved Andre Iguodala, the brilliant nihilist who couldn't help but preach and practice beautiful team basketball. Iguodala had out-performed his contracts. In Kerr's first season, Iguodala made a sacrifice by coming off the bench so that

Harrison Barnes, a worse, younger player, could start. Iguodala earned Finals MVP in the Warriors' first championship in forty years, to say nothing of many clutch playoff performances over the dynastic run. And, on June 30, 2019, when shit finally hit the fan, and Durant really did leave the franchise, the Warriors shipped Iguodala off to Memphis. Andre Iguodala may have been loved, but, at thirty-five, he was more loved than valued.

That day started with an announcement of an announcement. Newsmakers relayed that KD would announce his free agency decision on "The Boardroom" Instagram page. "The Boardroom" had been a fairly lame ESPN imitation of LeBron's more free-flowing *The Shop* on HBO, only with KD and a business spin. Whoever agreed to the show appeared to be under the misapprehension that fans were thrilling to hear athletes talk about investing in Postmates. The show had not been a hit, but could perhaps draw some adjacent publicity by releasing the info on its Instagram.

Not so much. Within a few hours those same news breakers tweeted that Kevin Durant was going to the Brooklyn Nets to join Kyrie Irving. This information had been released while Steph Curry was still in transit, from China, to meet with KD for one last talk. They met, in a cordial manner, hours after the news broke.

Good soldier Steph may have looked naive, but he appeared to the public, once again, as team oriented and well intentioned. KD, whatever the circumstances behind the news drop, looked like something else. Was this about Durant's anger? Or was it simply his method for detaching?

The public reception of the meeting was a microcosm of their dynamic. Durant had been irked by the positive coverage Curry received with such ease. On KD's final day as a Warrior, Curry, by just being dutiful Curry, received positive coverage at Durant's expense.

As Curry conferred with Durant, the Warriors Ops men were scrambling. Myers and Mike Dunleavy Jr. plotted in New York, where they'd arrived to pitch KD, while the rest of the Warriors team gathered together in Los Angeles. As the years have gone by, the league's gravity has shifted to LA It's where the players spend their offseasons and it's where the agents live. Though the NBA's official headquarters are in New York, they've about as much day-to-day influence on the sport as London had sway over Boston in the colonial era. New York offers occasional dictates from afar; LA directs on the ground level.

When Durant announced his intentions, the Warriors needed help from one particular LA-based agent, Aaron Mintz of CAA, whom they met with in Los Angeles shortly after the news came out. Mintz is not someone to be fucked with, if the Los Angeles Lakers' experience was any indication. After unceremoniously trading Mintz client D'Angelo Russell to Brooklyn in 2017, the Lakers were ultimately spurned by Paul George, another Mintz man, in 2018 free agency. For years, George was thought of as a sure thing for the Lakers. Instead, he shockingly chose to re-sign with Oklahoma City before eventually finagling a trade to the Clippers. Were the Russell trade and the spurning of Paul George connected? None of the principals would admit as much, but there's a reason that teams frequently do the bidding of the power agents.

Mintz was willing to play ball with the Warriors when it was decided that they pivot to a "sign and trade" for Russell. Durant's and Irving's arrival would mean the Nets couldn't pay Russell. By swapping Russell out to the Warriors, the Nets could at least recoup some value, while allowing the Warriors to invest in a twenty-three-year-old point guard with upside. To make the move financially possible, the Warriors had to unload Iguodala.

The move was understandable from the Warriors' perspective but perhaps illustrative of how the Warriors had become "just

like the other teams." Iguodala, in all his irascible wisdom, represented a Warriors team that was long on professionalism.

Russell might have been young and unlucky, but beyond the basketball, he was known for revealing his teammate's love affair on social media and a failed attempt at smuggling weed through the airport via an Arizona Iced Tea can. Will Cain, an ESPN TV commentator, mocked the latter pratfall, exclaiming, "This fool hid contraband inside contraband!"

But this was all the price of getting back in the big game. Russell would have a max contract, which paradoxically made him more valuable to the Warriors than if he came cheaper. For a trade to be possible under collective bargaining agreement rules, salaries must "match" on both sides within a certain range. Were Russell to have a quality season, he could be swapped for a possibly unhappy superstar who wanted out of his situation, thanks to the contract match.

This was how the league had moved. D'Angelo Russell was as much an asset as he was an investment, even if the Warriors had committed four years and over $117 million to him. He was an arbitrage mechanism as much as he was a stopgap measure for Klay Thompson's protracted absence.

Of course, nobody could admit this out loud. That's why the Warriors pushed back publicly on what everybody thought they knew. "We didn't sign him with the intention of trading him," Bob Myers insisted at a media session. Nobody believed this, but nobody had to. This was just how NBA kabuki goes.

Unless, it wasn't just kabuki. From conversations within the team and league, Bob Myers saw something in Russell's potential. Joe Lacob certainly saw value in opening up Chase Center with a young All-Star. The coaching staff? They were somewhere between shell-shocked and chagrined. Russell represented a division between Ops and coaching.

Lavish praise of the outgoing Kevin Durant might have been the real NBA kabuki move. It would look gauche, at the very least, if the Warriors were disrespectful to Durant for spurning them. Whatever the circumstances, KD had ruptured his Achilles under their jurisdiction. Why take shots and tempt the possibility of an ugly legal battle?

So the Warriors overcompensated. There was a hasty July 1 announcement that the Warriors would retire Kevin Durant's number.

Joe Lacob wrote in an official team statement, "As long as I am Co-Chairman of this team, no player will ever wear #35 for the Warriors again."

The NBA world was mostly confused by this, if not outright scoffing. Durant had played three seasons for the Warriors, great as they were. He was outwardly scornful in the last of them, and took a significant discount to leave. In his exit announcement, there was no offering of thanks to anyone associated with the Warriors, not even the fans. He had apparently spurned Curry's oceans-crossing entreaties.

Behind the scenes, the Warriors weren't exactly in a state of rapturous gratitude toward Kevin. For one, he kept intervening in the sign and trade, believing that his former team wasn't giving enough in the exchange. "We had the deal agreed to three times," one high-level Warriors Ops staffer said. "He fucked us." The Warriors were forced to eventually part with a potential first-round draft pick.

Joe Lacob still had to play the game, though. He might have delighted in standing over a vanquished Larry Ellison and beating his chest sans fear of the powerful man's reprisal, but Ellison was merely worth over $70 billion. He wasn't an NBA superstar. Kevin Durant, ruptured Achilles and all, was still an NBA superstar. He still made the rules, even for a team he'd left. The Warriors would

have to placate Kevin Durant, whichever jersey he wore. So long as he kept producing, the league writ large would have to as well. If his contracts stayed short, he might just choose your team as his next venture.

At Summer League 2019, in Las Vegas, Warriors rookies and roster hopefuls played before a crowd at the Thomas & Mack Center. D'Angelo Russell appeared and sat courtside next to power agent Aaron Mintz. The duo made their way over to the behind-basket area, where they schmoozed with the new bosses, Joe Lacob and Bob Myers. There was laughter and backslapping. Myers's diligent teen nephew was in the vicinity, working the Summer League event, fetching waters for all the power players. He wanted an eventual career in basketball, an existence that, for once, looked rather glamorous that evening.

Of course, nobody quite knew if Lacob and Myers were Russell's new bosses. If Russell faltered and lost value, Lacob and Myers retained their authority. If the twenty-three-year-old exceeded expectations and turned into a bona fide star of the future? Then Lacob and Myers would lose control and lose authority. They were hoping for this, even banking on their own usurpation. These were highly successful men whose hope was to be subservient to the whims of a twenty-something. In other words, they were at the top of the food chain in Basketball Ops.

Meanwhile, Iguodala had been knocked down a peg within his ecosystem. He could still command interest as a helpful veteran player, but for how much longer? Andre might have been braced for this moment, having known the others would never lead to happiness. "Something Obama said stuck with me," Iguodala had told me at his locker, late in the 2018–2019 season, when thinking back on the team's first White House visit. "All these billionaires, none of them are happy."

Months earlier I had asked Iguodala about the buzz that he might one day make the Hall of Fame. "I don't care," Iguodala responded. "None of it matters."

Iguodala offered the following take on the future, one that's either grim or liberating depending on your perspective. "See, here's how it works. One day, you're replaced. Then it's some other motherfucker in there. And then there's another motherfucker. And another after that. Nobody remembers anything. None of it matters!"

When asked about the importance of giving an emotional Hall of Fame speech, Iguodala said, "Does anyone remember any of those speeches other than Jordan's?"

True, almost nobody echoes across multiple generations. Even in the case of Jordan, after all the success, he's hardly a model of happiness. Jordan's aforementioned Hall of Fame speech is mostly famous for unnerving the audience with a slew of aired resentments. The apotheosis of sports success does not appear to correlate with the apotheosis of happiness.

Jordan's friend Charles Barkley, often mocked for never winning a championship, strikes a stark attitudinal contrast to His Airness. Barkley was a great player who perhaps never achieved ultimate glory because he enjoyed his work-life balance and meals on the road. Yet he's contagiously, hilariously happy in most settings. He gets paid to pontificate and joke around with friends on television. Barkley never won a ring, but he won retirement. The latter might have something to do with the former. Life never ended up revealing the lie of winning to Chuck.

I ran into Barkley in the summer of 2019, at 5 a.m. in Toronto Pearson International Airport. Barkley wore a hat, as famous people do for camouflage, a hilariously ineffective method considering Barkley's recognizable frame and tendency to do a booming

commentary on all he sees. After passing Customs, as he walked behind me, he bellowed of our path through the gift shops, "Oh, they WANT you to buy some shit here!"

I introduced myself and he remembered me from the KD press conference blowup. "Man, don't sweat it," Chuck said of Durant. "He's mad at everybody." Barkley, on the other hand, was feeling farthest from anger, or any negative emotion really. His contract afforded him a nice, lengthy vacation, on which he was about to embark. He was ecstatic, beaming as he counted up his weeks of zero responsibilities. As we got to his gate Barkley told me, "Well, I'm off to Puerto Rico to play golf. Have fun working, mother-fucker!" Chuck knew how to exist without the game that made him rich and famous. Barkley's playing career was long over, yet he was perpetually in his prime.

Meanwhile, I was still tethered in a way to this team that hadn't stopped, that still aspired to make history into a holding pattern. A month later, its grip on history slipped. Had the sun set on this particular dynasty? Probably. The sun had yet to set on a certain exiting superstar, however. He still commanded attention and fealty, even when on the mend. He had left the greatest team ever, but the sun's glow remained on Kevin Durant's attenuated frame, just never offering enough warmth to make a man comfortable.

ACKNOWLEDGMENTS

First, I want to thank my wife, Allie, for taking our baby on a vacation to Mexico so I could complete this book. The tales of flying alone with the boy were quite harrowing and I appreciate her sacrifice. Additionally, I just love her and I doubt I could write, much less be sane, without her in my life. I want to also thank my mother, who, in addition to being my mother, has been a brilliant thought partner on this journey. I am indebted to my agent, Kate McKean, who more or less conjured the idea of my writing this kind of book. Thank you so much to Benjamin Adams, Kelly Anne Lenkevich, Bill Warhop, and the team at Hachette for their incredible patience and guidance. I've been blown away by the work they've done in supporting a creative vision. This is an odd kind of project. Most sports books are celebratory in nature, but this one dwells on the sadness that comes with success. I quite appreciate how Hachette put their backing in a different kind of sports history.

So much of this book is informed by the work of my colleagues at *The Athletic*: Tim Kawakami, Marcus Thompson, and Anthony Slater. I'm lucky to work with not only my friends, but people who set an example of what I want to aspire to as a professional. I want

to extend an additional thank you to Marcus, who provided a few stories that made it into these pages. I've benefited tremendously from his idiosyncratic genius over the years. Speaking of idiosyncratic geniuses, a big thank-you goes out to *The Atlantic* podcast producer Jade Hoye, who's been a tireless muse, creative partner, and friend through the last decade. Finally, I would like to thank the Golden State Warriors and all who agreed to interviews within it. Maybe they won't like everything in this book, but I do appreciate their collective professionalism, work ethic, and willingness to be examined up close. Whatever people might say about the franchise, it's not an insecure organization.

ETHAN SHERWOOD STRAUSS is a senior NBA writer at the *Athletic* where he also hosts his *House of Strauss* podcast. His work has been cited in publications such as the *New York Times*, *Slate*, and *FiveThirtyEight*. In his first full-time season as a beat writer, he picked the Warriors to win their first title in forty years and they obliged. The following season, Ethan wrote "How Nike Lost Steph Curry to Under Armour," the most read NBA article in the English language of 2016. He currently lives in Oakland, California, with his wife and child.

PublicAffairs is a publishing house founded in 1997. It is a tribute to the standards, values, and flair of three persons who have served as mentors to countless reporters, writers, editors, and book people of all kinds, including me.

I. F. STONE, proprietor of *I. F. Stone's Weekly*, combined a commitment to the First Amendment with entrepreneurial zeal and reporting skill and became one of the great independent journalists in American history. At the age of eighty, Izzy published *The Trial of Socrates*, which was a national bestseller. He wrote the book after he taught himself ancient Greek.

BENJAMIN C. BRADLEE was for nearly thirty years the charismatic editorial leader of *The Washington Post*. It was Ben who gave the *Post* the range and courage to pursue such historic issues as Watergate. He supported his reporters with a tenacity that made them fearless and it is no accident that so many became authors of influential, best-selling books.

ROBERT L. BERNSTEIN, the chief executive of Random House for more than a quarter century, guided one of the nation's premier publishing houses. Bob was personally responsible for many books of political dissent and argument that challenged tyranny around the globe. He is also the founder and longtime chair of Human Rights Watch, one of the most respected human rights organizations in the world.

·   ·   ·

For fifty years, the banner of Public Affairs Press was carried by its owner Morris B. Schnapper, who published Gandhi, Nasser, Toynbee, Truman, and about 1,500 other authors. In 1983, Schnapper was described by *The Washington Post* as "a redoubtable gadfly." His legacy will endure in the books to come.

Peter Osnos, *Founder*